Charles Berlitz is the author of many books, including the world famous bestseller, *The Bermuda Triangle*. He is the grandson of the founder of the famous Berlitz language schools and is himself an accomplished linguist with a working knowledge of some thirty languages. An expert scuba diver, he has been able to combine his hobby with archaeological investigation and he has examined at first hand many of the strange ruins of lost civilizations which have been discovered beneath the sea.

By the same author

CHARLES BERLITZ

Mysteries from Forgotten Worlds

With contribution of photographs, drawings and field archaeology reports by J. Manson Valentine

GRANADA
London Toronto Sydney New York

Published by Granada Publishing Limited in 1983

ISBN 0 586 05646 7

First published in Great Britain by
Souvenir Press Ltd 1972
Copyright © Charles Berlitz 1972

Granada Publishing Limited
Frogmore, St Albans, Herts AL2 2NF
and
36 Golden Square, London W1R 4AH
866 United Nations Plaza, New York, NY 10017, USA
117 York Street, Sydney, NSW 2000, Australia
100 Skyway Avenue, Rexdale, Ontario, M9W 3A6, Canada
61 Beach Road, Auckland, New Zealand

Printed and bound in Great Britain by
Cox & Wyman Ltd, Reading
Set in Plantin

Granada ®
Granada Publishing ®

The author wishes to express his appreciation for the collaboration of J. Manson Valentine Ph.D., Curator Honoris of the Museum of Science of Miami and Research Associate of the Bishop Museum of Honolulu. Dr. Valentine brings to this book his long experience, findings and theories in prehistoric archaeology gained in expeditions in Central and South America, Fiji, Hawaii, New Zealand, Iceland, Lapland, North Africa, the Canary Islands, the West Indies, and the Bahamas, where he has pursued his search for lost cultures in jungles, mountains, caves and under the sea. A large proportion of the photographs in this book have been taken on his expeditions.

CONTENTS

MYSTERIES FROM FORGOTTEN WORLDS

CHAPTER ONE

THE UNEXPLAINED CIVILIZATIONS BEFORE HISTORY

Through his development of science Man now stands at the threshold of manned space exploration, with new planets to conquer—a situation somewhat equivalent to the Western Europeans in 1493 after Columbus found transatlantic voyages to be feasible. But, through the development of this same advanced science, Man may also be standing at five minutes to Armageddon. But whichever time or destiny slot we consider ourselves to be in, our education, traditions, and generally optimistic view of history have conditioned us to accept civilization's march forward. The advance of civilization fits into a neat pattern, starting in Mesopotamia and Egypt, developing religious and political perfections via Palestine, Syria, and Greece, legalistic and organizational perfection in the Roman Empire, retrogressing somewhat through the Middle Ages but plunging forward again in the Renaissance, the discovery of the New World and the Industrial Revolution.

The march of civilization seems to explain the increasing capabilities and organization of Man from earliest time to the present. However, as Man by his very scientific expertise is able to examine more completely traces of his own past, certain disquieting and disturbing elements have come to light, especially within the last few years. A somewhat iconoclastic question increasingly confronts the investigator of ancient history: is it possible that there were other civilizations in the long history of Man that we know nothing of, or of which we hear only vague echoes, often confused with cultures that are more or less familiar to us?

Our concept of ancient history was originally strongly influenced by our dependence on the Bible; of which the books specifically relating to the history of antiquity are written from an understandably insular point of view. This has tended to distort a general view of ancient cultures and completely neglect some important ones, including the Hittites and the Minoans, while at the same time preserving fascinating allusions to cultures of extreme and almost prehistoric antiquity, civilizations so far back in time and completely lacking in other references as to be classified as prehistory.

It is not necessarily to certain historic cultural oversights, races, and cultures neglected by the biblical writers and other commentators of recognized antiquity that we should address ourselves, but perhaps to older lost cultures of which these are merely the vestiges. Did the ancient Mayas, the pre-Incas of South America, the mound builders of North America, the astonishingly sophisticated cave artists of Western Europe and North Africa, the pre-Dynastic Egyptians, the population remnants of Easter Island and the Canary Islands, to name just a few, develop their culture themselves, or were they remnants of predawn cultures?

We now have at our command means of dating culture periods which tend to shake up our ideas of how long Man has been civilized. Contributing finds are constantly appearing from widely separated areas: a walled city at the site of Jericho has been dated back 10,000 years, almost within the time period of legendary 'Atlantis.' The established date for Jericho already goes several thousand years beyond the 4004 B.C. date for the beginning of the world, as established by James Usher, Archbishop of Armagh, Ireland, in 1650; a date which still subtly influences us in our consideration of the age of civilization. (Dr. John Lightfoot, Vice Chancelor of Cambridge, a contemporary of Bishop Usher, specified further that: 'Man was created by the Trinity on the 23rd of October, 4004 B.C. at nine o'clock in the morning.') Even more fantastic was an attempt by Philip Henry Gosse, as late as 1857, to justify biblical tradition in terms of fossils which were turning up in increasing quantities in the nineteenth century. Gosse, an outstanding authority on marine life, proposed that God had created fossils of extinct animals at the same time he created Adam and Eve.

While we of the atomic age are now well aware of the age of our planet as well as the approximate beginning of the Quartenary Era, the epic of man, dating back roughly 2,000,000 years, it is nevertheless true that our own generally accepted view of the age of 'civilization' curiously coincides with the biblical concept of the beginnings of man. The patent explanation is simply that we can ascribe civilization and history only to written records.

But even this foundation is changing. Paleolithic tool-cut notations carved in bone, calculated to be 30,000 years old, are now being studied in a new light, namely that they are records of lunar cycles and notations over long periods of the phases of the moon, a sort of 'cave-man' astronomy. That such apparent records are found in caverns in different sections of Europe tend to change our concept of the intellectual capacity of our cave-dwelling ancestors.

What appear to be letters or writing, or symbols preliminary to a form of written script have been discovered at sites in France and Spain which indicate that writing or symbolic writing should be dated backwards 8000 to 10,000 years. Cave paintings in Lussac, France, not open to public inspection, show men and women of predawn civilization dressed in comfortable clothes of surprisingly modern pattern, quite different from the furs and bones we usually associate with the cave peoples. And in Rhodesia a copper mine has been dated as having been worked 47,000 years ago, leading one to the observation that the unknown workers of the mine had a purpose and a use for the copper they were extracting. The farther we go back in history the more indications we find that there was a civilization of as yet undetermined scope which existed before the civilizations whose annals we possess, albeit somewhat incompletely.

It has long been a jibe of certain archaeologists and students of antiquity that if a highly developed and 'uncatalogued' civilization existed prior to the ones we know of, why is there no concrete record of it? It has also been suggested that if these prehistoric cultures were so civilized why have we not been able to turn up a single watch, fountain pen, or cigarette lighter among the digs? As if in answer to these 'in' quips, some rather amazing discoveries have been unearthed during the last few years, implying the knowledge and use of electricity by the ancients, measures of planetary distances, weights and volumes, a realistic concept of the earth, including a certain familiarity with the Antarctic continent thousands of years before it was officially 'discovered,' advanced knowledge of cartography and spherical geometry, the grinding of microscopic lenses, the use of computers and other scientific and mathematical knowledge heretofore unsuspected.

It is almost as if someone who was here before had left messages for us in the shape of certain key monuments and buildings which would help other races advanced enough to read them, for guidance and sometimes for a warning.

Some of these monuments still exist and some 'natural' features of terrain previously thought to be too big to be manmade may in reality be monuments of a most extraordinary nature. An outstanding example is the Great Pyramid of Egypt. The more we study and measure it the more its concept seems to change, becoming subtly different from what we had previously supposed. Was it simply a tomb—as Herodotus, the wandering Greek historian supposed? Or was it something else—an indication of the prime meridian for astronomers and cartographers who would one day forget why it was built? Was it a colossal equinoxial clock, a guide to planting and harvesting for the millions who farmed along the Nile? Was it a gigantic time capsule indicating, long before our Common Era that an elder race once knew about —the weight of the earth, the distance between the earth and the sun, a key to mathematics and the sidereal year, a guide to geography and cartography, and finally the repository of a prehistoric and up to now unsuspected standard system of measures?

The Great Pyramid is a landmark of the ancient past that is still with us. It is easy to recognize (it should be, at a height of 45 stories!) as a mass, perhaps less easy to recognize for what it really is. But over the world there are other monu-

14

ments less easy to recognize, some because they are so huge, such as the Panecillo, a small mountain outside of Quito, Ecuador, long thought to be a natural mountain but apparently man-made, as well as many other seemingly natural features in Mexico, Peru, Brazil, Europe, Central Asia, and even the Pacific Islands.

The methods and equipment now at the disposal of archaeologists are immeasurably superior to the inspired and dedicated diggings of the past. The new tools include the use of airplanes and aerial photography for spotting landsites, midget submarines, sonar and scuba divers for underwater exploration, radar and mine detector equipment as well as the cesium magnometer for subsoil investigation, an increased referral knowledge of ancient languages, much of it established on code-breaking procedures and an entire new science of restoring, cleaning, and re-emphasizing features of ancient artifacts and, most importantly, dating them, culminating in the Carbon-14 dating technique.

It is curious to reflect that most of the improvements in modern archaeological investigation owe their developments to modern warfare. Many air sightings were made by pilots on active duty in World Wars I and II and were subsequently explored. Air reconnaissance, for example, has identified the sunken harbor of Tyre and other ancient Mediterranean ports now under the sea. The street and canal plan of the lost Etruscan city of Spina, covered for centuries by marshes near Venice; the sunken pleasure city of Baiae, a sort of Roman Las Vegas, and numerous jungle covered Mayan cities in Central America and pre-Inca ruins in South America owe their rediscovery to the airplane. A single example illustrates the new view of the past we can get from the air: near Persepolis, Iran, four hundred unsuspected ancient sites were recorded in thirteen hours' flying time, and vertical aerial photographs of a nearby area showed in detail, through terrain pattern visible only from the air, a city plan an archaeological expedition had been trying to map for over a year and a half.

The tools of war therefore have immeasurably increased our

ability to locate and study ancient cultures, many of which owed their demise to war and conquest—rather a cogent commentary on the cyclic process of progress, war, devastation, and reawakening, such as we have observed in our own recorded history.

As we now examine the surface of the earth, its subsoil, the bottoms of lakes, seas, rivers, the continental shelves under the ocean, and even the abyss, we find increasing evidence not only of human habitation but of 'uncatalogued' cultures we know little or nothing about—which have disappeared for reasons yet unknown. In fact when we do study these cultural remains of what we assume to be primitive peoples the mystery deepens. How can we explain the Nazca area of coastal Peru where an entire desert is marked for hundreds of square miles with what appear to be cosmic charts, diagrams, and symbols and animals that can be seen and studied only from the air? One is inclined to speculate on some cultural connection with such places as the Great Zodiac of Glastonbury, England, laid out on a circle thirty miles in circumference, the carefully set enormous stones of Carnac, Brittany, Stonehenge on the Salisbury Plain, and even with the mysterious mounds of the Mississippi Valley and other places in the central United States; huge earthworks and pyramid mounds, making perfect circles, squares within circles, measured polygons, rhomboids, ellipses, and representations of animals and serpents not always evident from the ground level but perfect when seen from above.

The enormous pre-Inca walls of the stone temples on the Andean plateaus and mountains are inexplicable, not only for the method of transportation employed by the builders but also for the minutely exact and almost capricious fitting of many-angled granite blocks weighing hundreds of tons.

Since the invention of carbon dating which, unfortunately, does not date stone the approximate age of many 'unexplained' ruins has been tentatively established, sometimes with astonishing results, usually much greater than hitherto assumed. (The immense Glastonbury Zodiac was given an age of 15,000 years!) As dates of human cultural periods are pushed farther and farther back we find that we not only have left far behind the 'creation' of 4004 B.C. established by Bishop Usher (which, oddly enough, corresponds vaguely to a written history starting point in the Egypt–Sumeria area) but to put civilization back to a point during and *before* the last glaciation.

There are many other ways of calculating or establishing the age of artifacts or buildings, but the Carbon-14 dating method is the most usable at this time. Briefly, it is this: any organic material loses half its carbon every 5600 years—so that by reducing it in a reactor and weighing the remains, a tentative figure plus or minus a variable figure—usually 280 years—may be established. The only trouble being that this process demolishes the material or artifact being tested. Bearing in mind the B.C. dates we find in texts on Ancient History, a glance at some selected Carbon-14 dates are thought provoking.

	Approximate age in years with possible variant	
Altar—Stonehenge, England	1,846	±275
Pyramid Mound—Silbury Hill, Avebury, England	4,115	±95
Tools found in Western Iran	100,000	
Inhabited site, Star Carr, England	10,000	
Cave paintings, Lascaux, France	16,000	±900
Dead Sea Scrolls, Qumrun, Israel	2,005	±275
Remains of walled city of Jericho, Israel	8,800	
Cremation mound, Tara, Ireland	4,000	
Bones with 'Calendar' markings, Dordogne, France	30,000	
Mohenjo-Daro ruins, India	5,500	
Flute—Paracas, Peru	8,000	
Axes—Kalambo Falls, Malawi	56,300	
Sandles—Oregon, U.S.A.	9,053	±350
Cotton Fabric, Huaca Prieta, Peru	4,515	
Iron mine—Ngwenya, Swaziland	43,000	
Mystery Hill, Massachusetts, U.S.A.	2,970	

Before Carbon-14 testings, some of these dates were already assumed and the tests tended to confirm them, but others tend to push prehistory back at an increasingly vertiginous rate. The 43,000-year-old iron mine, for one example, strongly implies that our prehistoric predecessors were not so brutish as we supposed.

In the many thousand years between the advent of inventive and artistic Crô-Magnon man there is a space interval that could, if we could locate it, contain many centuries of culture and civilization. A vague memory of these has perhaps come down to us in the guise of legends of the great flood, common to almost all ancient peoples, and also as traditions of the recurring destruction of mankind (usually brought about by divine castigation of man's wickedness) by flood, fire, earthquakes, volcanic eruptions, or ice. Whatever may have been the reason for the persistence of these implied warnings, such as a technique of the priestly caste to preserve morality and obedience, these legends are so prevalent and widespread that they seem logically to be race memories of changes in the surface of the earth; cataclysms, ice ages, tremendous volcanic explosions and engulfing floods, when mountain ranges rose and lands sank beneath the sea.

From ancient India to ancient America through all the intervening lands going both ways around the world we find this same pattern of recurring catastrophes that almost wiped out mankind leaving on earth but a few survivors who escaped the common doom by hiding in caves, seeking refuge on high mountains, or floating it out in boats or arks. In most traditional cases the survivors comprised one chosen man, accompanied by one or more women, sometimes with whole families and sometimes with a selection of animals and birds, varying in species according to the part of the earth where the legend was current. In each case the survivors returned to start afresh the difficult upward climb to civilization.

The catastrophe is sometimes considered to have been a world-wide flood as in the Judeo-Christian tradition, a concept shared with the ancient Middle East, to a whole series of cataclysms as in the case of the traditions of India, where the god Vishnu, the Preserver, has periodically rescued mankind from nine great disasters and will eventually rescue him from the tenth. In ancient Mexico, the Toltecs calculated that the world had ended, or almost ended, three times and incorporated this belief into their calendar plan, later adopted by the Aztecs. According to Toltec calendar tradition the first age of earth was called the Water Sun, and the earth was destroyed by floods; the second age was the Earth Sun, when the world was destroyed by earthquakes; the third era was the Wind Sun, when the destruction was caused by cosmic winds. We are still in the fourth age, which is called the Fire Sun, and this one is due to end with a tremendous and general conflagràtion, a rather informed guess fully shared by some of our own prophets of atomic doom.

This theory of periodic catastrophes causing new civilizations to start with a more or less clean slate was generally accepted and often commented on in the ancient world, although seldom so lucidly as by Plato, the Greek philosopher who made use of it in his dialogue called *Timaeus*. Plato is describing the visit of his distinguished ancestor, Solon, the Athenian lawgiver, philosopher, and scholar, with some Egyptian priests in the temple of Neith, in Saïs, Egypt. Solon is represented as discussing with the priests the antiquity of lineage of his family when one of the priests 'of very great age' seized the moment to deliver a lecture on antiquity, the importance of ancient records, and the recurring catastrophes of the earth. The words of Plato, coming down to us more or less as he said them more than 2000 years ago, afford a vivid commentary on antiquity before antiquity and the recurring cycles of civilization.

The Egyptian priest is reported to have said: 'O Solon, O Solon, you Hellenes are but children, and there is never an old man who is an Hellene ... in mind you are all young; there is no old opinion handed down among you by ancient tradition, nor any science which is hoary with age. And I will tell you the reason of this: there have been, and there will be again, many destructions of mankind arising out of many causes.

'There is a story which even you have preserved, that once upon a time Phaëthon, the son of Helios, have yoked the steeds in his father's chariot, because he was not able to drive them in the path of his father, burnt up all that was upon the earth, and was himself destroyed by a thunder-bolt. Now, this has the form of a myth, but really signifies a declination of the bodies moving around the earth and in the heavens, and a great conflagration of things upon the earth recurring at long intervals of time: when this happens, those who live upon the mountains and in dry and lofty places are more liable to destruction than those who dwell by rivers or on the sea-shore; and from this calamity the Nile, who is our never-failing savior, saves and delivers us.

'When, on the other hand, the gods purge the earth with a deluge of water, among you herdsmen and shepherds on the mountains are the survivors, whereas those of you who live in cities are carried by the rivers into the sea; but in this country neither at that time nor at any other does the water come from above on the fields, having always a tendency to come up from below, for which reason the things preserved here are said to be the oldest.

'... And whatever happened either in your country or in ours, or in any other region of which we are informed—if any action which is noble or great, or in any other way remarkable has taken place, all that has been written down of old, and is preserved in our temples; whereas you and other nations are just being provided with letters and the other things which States require; and then, at the usual period, the stream from heaven descends like a pestilence, and leaves only those of you who are destitute of letters and education; and thus you have to *begin all over again as children*, and know nothing of what happened in ancient times, either among us or among yourselves.

'As for those genealogies of yours which you have recounted to us, Solon, they are no better than the tales of children; for, in the first place, you remember one deluge only, whereas there were many of them ...'

CHAPTER TWO

CRYPTIC MESSAGES FROM THE PAST

Is there any tangible proof that an advanced civilization or civilizations existed before our own recorded beginnings? When we consider the results and implications of new archaeological techniques in pushing back the 'time curtain' there certainly has been time for various civilizations to have existed as a prologue to our own. These cultures would certainly have been different from ours, with emphasis perhaps on certain patterns that we do not yet perceive. However, in examining such a theory we should consider, given the possibility of a developed civilization somehow having existed in the neolithic era or prior to the melting of the last glaciers, whether or not something would have survived that we could examine in the light of present scientific knowledge. Given the time lapse in question—8000 to 15,000 years ago or even earlier it would be a wonder if anything survived at all. Sir Charles Lyell, a nineteenth-century British scholar and student of ancient man neatly phrased the 'establishment' point of view when he commented, re prehistoric artifacts being examined at that time:

Instead of the rudest pottery or flint tools, so irregular in form as to cause the unpracticed eye to doubt whether they afford unmistakable evidence of design, should we not be finding sculptured forms surpassing in beauty the masterpieces of Phidias or Praxiteles; lines of buried railway and electric telegraphs, from which the best engineers of our day might gain invaluable hints; astronomical instruments and microscopes of more advanced construction than any known in Europe, and other indications of perfection in the arts and sciences, such as the nineteenth century has not yet witnessed? Still farther would the triumphs of inventive genius be found to have been carried when the later deposits, now assigned to the ages of bronze and iron, were formed. Vainly should we be straining our imagination to guess the possible uses and meanings of such relics—machines, perhaps for navigating the air or exploring the depths of the oceans or for calculating arithmetical problems beyond the wants or even the conceptions of living mathematicians.

Sir Charles's observation is in accord with the traditional and somewhat logical reasoning of: 'If there had been developed civilizations anterior to ours, why haven't we found anything concrete indicating even an approach to the artifacts and techniques of modern civilizations—even a watch, a cigarette lighter, or a transistor radio?'

But perhaps our prehistoric cultural predecessors had a different form of technical development which we have been unable to identify. However, in the intervening years some rather unusual discoveries have been made, some among which would almost provide a direct answer to Sir Charles, who is now either in a position of total knowledge or total disinterest. In any case, his ideological descendants are faced with the problem of revising to a great extent our concept of the knowledge and development of extreme antiquity. Artifacts and copies of documents have been discovered, often in very unlikely places, subsequently put into museums and catalogued and then, after some years, re-examined and partially identified for what they really are.

For, when we consider the development of certain scientific knowledge current in the ancient past, a knowledge that seemed to decrease rather than increase through the centuries until the Renaissance, we experience a unique and strangely familiar feeling that somebody—a race or races—was here before history started. One forms the impression that much of our present knowledge of the world was known before and then forgotten or restricted in use through recorded history until it began to be rediscovered in our own era, beginning

22

perhaps in 1453, with the fall of Constantinople, the last repository of ancient culture.

Did this prehistoric race leave any traces except for some cyclopean walls and buildings, scattered throughout the earth and under the sea, whose construction we cannot even today explain without the use of modern machinery? We may have some such messages at hand, either as artifacts, recopied manuscripts, or recopied maps, since the originals would have long since disintegrated. These 'messages,' of course, were not designed specifically for the descendants, for we must remember that no matter how ancient the past may seem to us, to the people who lived in it it was *now*, and such records as they made were for their own use, except for the records of kings and emperors, preoccupied with their 'place in history.' They are, nevertheless, a form of communication or message and, to some of those who attempt to interpret them, they seem to say: 'Yours is not the first world's civilization nor are the cultures you consider to be your own roots the true beginning. Thousands of years ago we already knew what you have only recently discovered—the shape and size of the world and its relation to the cosmos. We had telescopes, lenses, computers, a knowledge of mathematics and the concept of matter. We traveled all over a younger world, when the great icefields still covered the north and when the seas of the southern polar continent were still navigable and parts of the land were free of ice. We left detailed maps of the continents we visited, of which the very memory was lost in the intervening centuries. Younger races, after we disappeared, retained some of our knowledge, a knowledge which has helped you build your own world, even now in danger of destruction.'

Messages that come from the very distant past come in different forms. They should be considered first in the light of transmitted knowledge—some of which has been misinterpreted or is still unrecognized—but other material, such as ancient maps, has come down to us from remote antiquity and, according to strong indications, helped in the discovery of the New World. In other words, Columbus, through these maps from an age unknown, may have known where he was going.

Columbus is thought to have had at his disposal maps or copies of maps used by the navigators of classical antiquity, the Minoans, Phoenicians, Carthaginians, Greeks, and Romans and by people who preceded them as world travelers. Some of these maps were recently rediscovered and others existed but were not realized to be what they really were— parts of superior world maps drawn with a knowledge of spherical trigonometry as applied to map projections before trigonometry was invented and before it was generally known that the world was round.

These maps were apparently used and copied by succeeding generations of mariners and used as maritime route maps, vastly superior to the authoritative world maps of antiquity and the Middle Ages. From the mariner's point of view they had to be, in as much as they represented to seafarers a means of survival rather than general and picturesque information. The originals from which these maps were copied were destroyed or lost in the burnings and lootings of the great library centres of classic times although several of them reappeared after the fall of Constantinople.

These copies of copies seem to indicate, as can be crosschecked by comparing them with modern maps from the point of view of latitude, longitude, and comparative distances between identifiable locations which had been set forth in remarkable and convincing detail in Professor Charles Hapgood's study, *Maps of the Ancient Sea Kings*, that the cartographers who first drew them were familiar not only with the 'known' world but the *world*. They were able to map the coastlines of the Americas, the mountains of South America, and the coasts and interior of Antarctica, centuries before either were officially discovered. Even more incredibly, notably in the Piri Reis map from Istanbul, dated 1513, topographical features of the Antarctic continent are correctly shown although they are now under thousands of feet of ice and have presumably been so covered for many thousands of years.

Some world travelers were familiar with the shape of the earth, could find their way around it, and drew maps of America and the Caribbean more than two thousand years before Columbus proved they existed and, in like manner, visited and mapped Antarctica many centuries before Captain Cook 'proved' in the eighteenth century, that Antarctica did not exist.

The appearance of the Antarctic continent on world maps prior to its discovery can be explained by fifteenth century cartographers in order to fill in unknown sections of the world, using maps that had survived from very ancient times. This frequently gave the extraordinary result that the unknown regions, copied and recopied from ancient times, were often more correct than regions more or less familiar to the map makers. The 1538 Mercator map of the little known west coast of South America was more correct than the 1569 map he made when the west coast had been better explored. An impelling reason for Captain Cook's journey in search of the Antarctic continent was the very fact that it appeared on so many maps, and his erroneous conclusion about it not existing was, of course, simply because he did not sail far enough to the south.

One may wonder why a person of the scientific attainments of Ptolemy (Claudius Ptolemaeus), Custodian of the Library of Alexandria in the second century A.D., and author of the famous *Geographica*, of such great influence in antiquity, could have substantially correct maps of the world at his disposal, as they must have been, and still not use them. The answer is probably that he simply considered them interesting theories but concluded that they were incorrect and, basing his own maps on mileage calculated by the 'pedometer' method of the Roman legions who actually paced determined distances from point to point, was able to measure latitudes but, lacking a chronometer or like instrument, could not measure longitudes.

The Piri Reis map of 1513 which, according to its cartographer, Piri Reis, a former Turkish pirate who became an admiral, is apparently only a part of a world map made by him and based on maps going back hundreds of years before Ptolemy, who made famous though less exact world maps of his own when he was Custodian of Records at the Library of Alexandria about 2000 years ago.

The rediscovery of the Piri Reis map concerns a startling series of coincidences.

This ancient illustrated map, drawn on a gazelle hide, was found in 1929 in cleaning up the accumulation of ages in the harem of the Topkapi Palace in Istanbul, the former Constantinople, several years after the Turks, under Mustapha Kemal, had 'relieved' the former Sultan of his duties, his palaces and his harem. It seemed at first to be simply an interesting old map of the coasts of Spain, Africa, and South America, but an unexpected written reference to Columbus projected it into world news as a possible connection to Columbus's 'lost map' used on his first crossing of the Atlantic. It said, in part, referring to the Caribbean Islands:

... it is reported thus; that a Genoese infidel, his name was Colombo, he it was who discovered these places. For instance, a book fell into the hands of said Colombo, and he found it said in this book that at the end of the Western Sea, that is, on its western side, there were coasts and islands and all kinds of metals and also precious stones...

Besides this contemporaneous reference to Columbus, the map, unlike others of the time, showed correct longitudes. Copies of the map were circulated in world libraries and commented on in the international press. The U.S. Secretary of State, Henry L. Stimson, on reading about it in the *London News* and perhaps in consideration of the somewhat proprietary interest in Columbus felt in the U.S., requested the Turkish government to research the matter. An unsuccessful search was made, presumably in the reconverted harem, for the lost Columbus map and the missing part or parts of the Piri Reis map thereupon the matter was dropped. A seemingly minor item overlooked at the time was the notation by Piri Reis that in compiling his map he had used old charts and world maps 'drawn in the days of Alexander, Lord of the Two Horns, which show the inhabited quarter of the world ...' Apparently certain maps were rescued by individuals from the general destruction of the records of antiquity and thereafter used by Arab and Turkish mariners and later by Europeans as well. These seafaring maps contained a message that would be recognized only some time later.

Another copy of this map was given by a visiting Turkish naval captain to the U.S. Navy Hydrographic office in Washington, where it eventually found its way to the desk of Captain Arlington Mallery, an archaeologist and student of old maps especially the controversial Norse maps of Greenland and the Northern Ocean which definitely proved (to Scandinavians if not to the Latin peoples), that the Vikings discovered America.

When he received the Piri Reis map, Mallery, by a curious but understandable coincidence, was actually examining a copy of the *Geographic Journal* showing the glacier profile of Greenland. On the same page was a description and comparison of the Polar icecaps of the Arctic and Antarctic. Examining the bottom coastline of the Piri Reis map he concluded that it showed the coast of Queen Maud Land properly where it should be, and even its bays and islands, but *without the ice* which now covers them.

Professor Charles Hapgood, an archaeologist, historian, and cartographer, undertook a research program lasting for several years and involving many other maritime 'road maps' of antiquity, copied from ancient originals. Complete correlation of map features with modern maps indicated that the originals could not have been drawn without a knowledge of techniques unknown even in the Renaissance (the chronometer, necessary to determine longitude, was not known until about 1780) to say nothing of the difficulty of making ground surveys in the Antarctic.

When one examines the portion of the Piri Reis map that has survived, one is struck by the peculiar elongation of the South American coastline, although otherwise basically correct in its shape. This apparent discrepancy is, of course, an effective proof of the validity of this ancient map in that it attempts to project the round shape of the earth on a flat surface, taking as the prime meridian for the purpose of the map that of Syene, Egypt. Any modern spheroid projection on a flat surface would cause the same distortion. It is remarkable that ancient cartographers, at an unknown date in the past, not only knew about the coast of Antarctica but were familiar with the principle of spheroid projection (and we do not know how many times the map was imperfectly copied).

Points of reference of the Arctic coastline appear to be surprisingly and inexplicably exact. In the words of U.S.A.F.

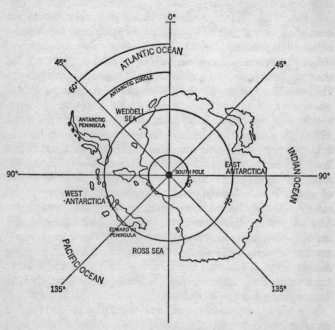

Sketch map of Antarctica as it would appear without the ice-cap, now more than two miles thick. The Antarctic continent, without the ice, would not be one land mass but two, separated by water.

(S.A.C.) Westover Air Force Base letter, elicited by Professor Hapgood for an appreciation, from the viewpoint of aerial survey, of his conclusions regarding the Piri Reis map: '... The geographical detail shown in the lower part of the map agrees very remarkably with the results of the Seismic profile made across the top of the icecap by the Swedish–British–Norwegian Antarctic Expedition of 1949. This indicates that the coastline had been mapped before it was covered by the icecap. The icecap in this region is now about a mile thick. We have no idea how the data on this map can be reconciled with the supposed state of geographical knowledge in 1513.'

Some of the information of the old sea maps, although decorated with drawings of mermaids, monsters, and wind-blowing cherub faces, implies that the original cartographers either had a detailed knowledge of the earth or were incredible guessers. One of the maps studied, by the French academician, Philippe Buache (1737), shows a waterway *across* Antarctica, which, if there were no ice, would divide Antarctica in two, a split not known until the International Geophysical Year 1958. With the aid of the most modern ice sounding devices it is now possible to ascertain that if the ice were not there East Antarctica would be separated from West Antarctica along the line of the Transantarctic Mountains, making much of which is now Marie Byrd Land part of a sea in the Byrd subglacial basin and finally uniting the Weddell and Ross Seas. Although the continent of Antarctica looks like one icy mass, we know, or accept on the faith we have in our recording devices, that it is really two gigantic islands. But how did the makers of the original maps consulted by Buache know this, hundreds or perhaps thousands of years before Antarctica was officially 'discovered.'

The section of the Orance Finné world map made in 1532 showing the Antarctic continent, not discovered until 1818, depicts rivers where there are now glaciers. The Ibn ben Zara map of the Mediterranean and Aegean Seas is seemingly accurate as to coastlines but shows—along with known islands—a number of islands that do not exist, or *no longer*

29

The Philippe Buache map of Antarctica, made in Paris in 1737, a century before Antarctica was discovered. Evidently copied from maps surviving from ancient times, it shows Antarctica as two separate land masses, a fact not established until the Geophysical Year of 1958 through ice soundings, but evidently known to navigators of prehistory, who may have visited Antarctica before it was covered by ice.

exist above water, as they perhaps did during the end of the last glaciation when the water level of the world was considerably lower. This latter supposition is borne out by what are apparently receding ice fields in Central Europe, England, and Ireland. And another excursion into the far past occurs in a Turkish map of 1559, the Hadji Ahmed, which not only shows the west coast of the Americas, but apparently indicates a land bridge between Siberia and Alaska—a suggestion that Hadji Ahmed's source presumably stems from the end of the last Ice Age, when the American Indians and assorted animals were trudging across what would later be the Bering Strait to the satisfaction of the later 'Asiatic origin' of the American school of anthropologists.

Professor Hapgood's work is thought-provoking and convincing, especially so as one is able, through comprehensive use of the tables of comparisons of longitude and latitude, and geometrical projections, to check the information oneself —a sort of do-it-yourself project in archaeological research, resulting in a rather convincing conclusion. To use Professor Hapgood's own words: 'In Greek times mathematics was in advance of mechanical instrumentation: There was no instrument for easily and correctly determining the longitude of places. However, the Piri Reis and the other maps we went on to study, seemed to suggest that such an instrument *had* once existed and had been used by people who knew very closely the correct *size* of the earth. They seem to have been quite well acquainted with the Americas, and to have mapped the coasts of Antarctica.'

In the *Popul Vuh*, a chronicle of the Maya Indians of Central America that has been handed down from antiquity there exists an unusual allusion peculiarly appropriate to the concept of a former world culture. It refers to '... the first race, capable of all knowledge ... examined the four corners of the horizon, the four points of the firmament and the round circles of the earth.'

Sometimes changes in our concepts of the technical development of lost ages are brought about by one small artifact —something like the cultural shock we would experience in finding an ancient cigarette lighter or flashlight. Usually the artifact has been gathered up with others, placed in some museum and labeled 'ritual object' or, in a burst of frankness, 'artifact; use unknown.'

Archaeologists and amateur archaeologists (the word 'amateur' has unfortunately developed an unfavourable connotation in archaeological and historical disciplines) have often speculated on some of these unidentified objects and sometimes they have identified them in a most surprising manner.

A German engineer, Wilhelm Konig, was contracted by the city of Baghdad in 1936 for a sewer construction project. He had noted and speculated on some flat stones and vases in the Baghdad museum classified as 'ritual objects.' Later he found in a ruined building about 1700 years old a vase with an inner cylinder of copper which was coated on the inside with asphalt. As he stated in a subsequent report: 'A thick plug of asphalt was forced into the upper end of the cylinder. In the centre of the plug was a solid piece of iron.' In effect this was an electric battery.

We do *not* know whether such an invention implies a more general use of electricity in ages when we are fairly certain that electricity was unknown, or whether it represents merely a technique for gold plating of jewelry for which it was and has since been used in the Middle East. In any case it is a tantalizing indication of possible ancient use of electricity thousands of years before Benjamin Franklin and his kite.

This indication that electricity was once used in Mesopotamia for jewelry for the adornment of women reminds one of the importance of the feminine mystique in developing civilization: mankind's earliest recorded mine, the Ngwenya 43,000 year old iron mine, was apparently mined for hematite ore, for use in cosmetics.

Something that looks like electroplating also has been found in the pre-Inca Chimú culture of ancient Peru, where diggings at Chan Chan, on the coastal plain have revealed beautiful artifacts made of *copper* but plated with gold or silver or made of silver and plated with gold. It is difficult to imagine how this could have been done without electrolysis although it has been suggested that some other process was employed which caused gold or silver fumes to arise from the molten metal and adhere to the copper. It is important to remember that this technique whichever it was came from an older culture than that found by the Spanish conquistadores, the later culture, to the satisfaction of the Spaniards, used solid gold and silver for their artifacts.

Whether or not electricity was ever used for lighting at some remote epoch is not known. There do exist some curious references to a knowledge of or implied familiarity with its effects which have come down to us in descriptions of the Temple of Solomon (cf. *Histoire Inconnue des Hommes:* Robert Charroux) whereby the temple had twenty-five long pointed iron rods set along its golden roof as well as water conductors leading to cisterns. Another reference to lightning comes from 400 B.C. from the Greek physician Ctesias, who speaks of the use in Egypt of 'metal swords' set in the ground, point upward, to avert the effects of storms.

In addition there seems to be a certain mystery connected with ancient or prehistoric illumination, besides the use of wood fires, torches, candles, oil lamps, or pitch braziers. As John Pfeiffer put it, referring to the use of fire, 'the lights went on about 750,000 years ago,' and since then, until modern illumination, all sorts of methods have been tried, including indirect lighting in the classical world and the magnification of light in the ancient Orient. But some questions remain unanswered. We may wonder how the subterranean painted and carved galleries of the Egyptian tombs, notably the exactly cut passages *under* the Great Pyramid of Gizeh, Egypt, could have been worked on without some effective form of illumination, especially since there are no marks on the low ceilings indicating the then known forms of lighting.

One is reminded of somewhat similar mystery in the Inca and pre-Inca ruins of South America, where low ceilings and passageways show no evidence of smoke blackening. In addition, recurring reports from several hundred years ago to the present day, from 'untamed' Indians from the upper tributaries of the Amazon, a vast region under a green sea of trees that may be as unexplored as any part of the earth, suggest that lost 'white' tribes are still inhabiting cyclopean cities from which strange lights shine at night from out the stone windows. Colonel Fawcett, a British explorer and writer, and others as well, considered these to be remnants of an ancient culture which had conserved, among other thinrgs, a lost knowledge of illumination held by their predecessors. Colonel

Fawcett was on an expedition tracking down one of these lost cities in the 1920s when he disappeared and, through repeated attempts of other expeditions to find *him*, finally ended up as a legend himself.

The Americas, North, South, and Central, and the Islands of the Caribbean Sea, are a most fruitful source of what one might term messages from the past, except that the past is generally more difficult to date in the absence of a written history and also since many of the artifacts we have at hand are of precious metals, stone and clay, which cannot be dated. A fascinating aspect of American archaeology, and one which has a bearing, though uncertain, on its age, is the fact that extinct animals are consistently depicted in the shape of mounds, as colossal stone statues, drawn on pottery, incised on rocks, on bas-reliefs of temples, or in the shape of artifacts.

In the United States, the shape of an elephant or mammoth can be clearly discerned in the Elephant Mound of Wisconsin, when considered from above, while something closely resembling an elephant's head with raised trunk occurs in architectural remains in Palenque, Mexico, as well as 'elephant' masks in Aztec sculpture. In Colombia incised drawings of elephants on golden discs have been recovered from an airport construction site near Cali (one is reminded of the existence of an elephant or mastodon 'graveyard' near Bogotá usually dated before the advent of civilized man in the world). In Brazil accurate likenesses of rhinoceroses have been found carved on rocks in the Amazon region as well as drawings of something that looks like a dinosaur. Rocks and cliffs carved into shapes resembling lions, hippopotamuses and other regionally unlikely animals exist in the Marcahuasi Plateau of Peru, while pottery found at Tiahuanaco of uncertain age (estimates of Tiahuanaco's age vary from 3000 to 12,000 years) furnish good representations of the extinct toxodon, a hippopotamus-like animal of prehistoric times, an indication that the people who drew it may possibly have seen it.

An extraordinary and mysterious system of ground markings exists in the Nazca Valley of Peru, north and south of the town of Nazca, about 250 miles south of Lima. It consists of a series of parallel and cross markings, resembling roads or delineations of directional paths, long referred to as 'Inca roads' except that unlike the remarkable real Inca road system they do not logically lead any place but form a maze of trapezoids, triangles, rectangles, and other geometrical shapes or straight lines with no discernible pattern. Other paths, when seen from above, form enormous figures of birds, spiders, turtles, jaguars, monkeys, snakes, fish, including a whale, a gigantic human figure, and other designs of things unknown. They were made by an unknown race, well before the advent of the Incas, perhaps fifteen centuries ago, by making furrows in the hard earth, scraping designs on the rock, and also by building small continuous hillocks, according to the terrain. Huge pictographs had been noted on the valley walls of the vicinity previously but the full impact of the Nazca 'lines' or 'roads' was not realized until they were first recurrently seen from the air during a series of irrigation studies. They are barely discernible from the ground. When you drive through Nazca on the Pan-American Highway you pass through a cluster of these 'roads,' but there is little to see.

From the air, however, the prospect is considerably different and this amazing complex of designs and figures can only be appreciated from above, where it can still be clearly seen after the intervening centuries.

The lines and enormous pictographs cover an area more than 60 miles long and at times, including markings on the slopes of the adjoining hills and mountains, more than 10 miles deep. The straight lines are exactly straight, as if expertly surveyed, a further inexplicable feature when we consider the relative size, place, and period of history. But the directional progress of these lines is no less mysterious. Sometimes they continue for several yards only and other times continue for miles, remaining absolutely straight while jumping over (or through) a mountain.

A great deal has been written about and speculated on concerning the possibility of these lines being 'prehistoric landing fields' for interstellar pilots, or even messages to cosmic travelers, a flight into fantasy which, oddly enough, finds an echo in ancient Peruvian tradition in a legend about the goddess Orejona landing in a great ship from the skies.

A somewhat less exciting although still fascinating explanation is suggested by the investigations of Dr. Paul Kosok and Dr. Maria Reiche. Dr. Kosok, while examining the mysterious lines *in situ*, happened to be standing on a hill, at the end of a large line from which others radiated. The date was June 22 —being the winter solstice below the equator. When the sun set it touched the horizon over the base of the line on which he and his wife were standing. This remarkable coincidence led him to check many other lines for astronomical direction and his findings indicated that many of the lines gave clear readings understandable to an astronomer, relating to the paths of the planets, the sun and moon and calculations relative to the solstices and equinoxes. Dr. Reiche, also through on-the-spot investigation, corroborated and elaborated these findings and even established a tentative date (A.D. 500) for the laying out of this 'world's largest astronomy book' by the process of establishing the yearly rate of deviation of elected 'fixed' stars from the paths traced in the desert.

Were these huge astronomy charts made for someone to see from above? If they were, the 'someone' would most likely be the gods who had to be reminded and placated so that they would not only keep the sun, moon, planets, and constellations on their roads or paths but keep the climate functioning as well. The enormous figures perhaps represented constellations of the zodiac or other star groups.

For ancient America was thoroughly preoccupied with its duty to the heavens in order to keep them working. Tribes and nations considered themselves responsible for the proper operation of the cosmos—the centre of Inca cosmology was the *Intihuatana*—'the hitching post of the sun,' a stone marker where the sun's shadow had exactly to fit during the solstice. The most ancient American cultures were those most concerned with astronomy and mathematical calculations; only later did the Aztecs tend to maintain the balance of heaven by constantly increasing numbers of human sacrifices, a payment which, as the Aztecs later found out, was not acceptable.

These enormous constructions, products of culturally advanced people who disappeared *before* the discovery of America, are repeated in other parts of the Americas. Almost 200 miles farther south, thousands of somewhat similar figures, including stars, are to be found engraved on rocks and cliffs as well as in California, on the Colorado River, where pictographs exist covering many acres of ground and consisting of rows and ridges of scraped small stones, corresponding closely to the Nazca techniques and including enormous human figures. It was called the Mojave Maze although the surviving Mojave Indians disclaimed any knowledge about it. A large part of it was destroyed in the 1880s when a railroad was built through it.

Perhaps the most striking of these ancient markings is the Candelabra of the Andes, an 800-foot-long carving in a towering cliff at Paracas, Peru, in the Bay of Pisco, which can be clearly seen from far out in the Pacific. This enormous carving resembles a candelabra, trident, or pitchfork and seems to point toward the Nazca Valley like a gigantic road sign. When the Spanish conquerors first noted it they took it to be a sign from heaven—the Trinity—and interpreted it as an encouraging 'go-ahead' signal for them to conquer, Christianize, and enslave the local inhabitants.

Upon examination of this 800-foot rock carving the Spaniards found that a huge rope was attached to the central fork and that there were indications that other cords and ropes, connected to the outer two arms, comprised some sort of apparatus of unknown use.

Robert Charroux suggests (cf. *Histoire Inconnue des Hommes Depuis Cent Mille Ans*) an explanation offered by a Peruvian commentator—Beltrán García. Beltrán García thinks that the 'Candelabra' may have been a tidal calculator but also '... [this] system, equipped with counterweights, graded ladders and ropes sliding on pulleys constituted a gigantic and precise seismograph, able to register telluric waves and seismic shocks coming not only from Peru but from all over the planet ...'

Other commentators have indulged in 'heavier-than-air' flights of fancy which would make the Paracas 'Candelabra' an aerial signpost pointing to the 'landing fields' of Nazca.

Like an exotic echo to such suppositions, an ancient South American artifact, approximately 1000 years old and strongly resembling an airplane of recent design eventually turned up in the Banco de Colombia collection of golden artifacts. When it was exhibited in the U.S. it caught the attention of Dr. Ivan Sanderson, biologist, archaeologist and author. The unidentified object in question looked like some sort of moth or other insect or a flat fish but, on high power lens inspection, Dr. Sanderson thought that it could be a representation of a mechanical rather than a natural object.

Dr. Sanderson who, as a biologist, was familiar with how insects or fish *should* look, became increasingly interested in the artifact which, while certainly resembling an airplane, also included its minor attributes while *not* including those of known fish, birds, or insects. For example, from the edges of the delta-like wings there was something clearly resembling mechanical ailerons or elevators. The body of the insect or fish, while missing most of its head where the head should be, did have a rectangular front end 'like an old-fashioned Rolls-Royce.' The tail was not simply upright like a fish tail but flanged like the tail on modern planes, and, if it *were* a plane, there seemed to be an indented seat at a point where a cockpit would normally be.

Further informed opinion came from other engineering authorities among whom was J. A. Ulrich, fighter pilot, engineer, and a pioneer pilot of German rocket planes. Ulrich was of the opinion, without having been previously informed as to what it was, that the mysterious golden object was an F-102 fighter and, noting that the wings curved down a little at the end, as is necessary for 'super-power abrupt rise' aircraft, that the shape of the plane '... spells out one thing—jet.' He observed that the rudder was conventional and that features at the end of the model might be speed brakes instead of elevators; the lack of rear elevators being a shared feature with the new Swedish SAAB aircraft.

Since gold cannot be closely dated there is always the possibility that the tiny airplane might be 'intrusive'; that is, placed accidentally or by design into a later find from another more recent epoch. All sorts of modern inventions of course, find their way into primitive reproductions, from the New Guinea natives who believe they were visited by gods who descended from the skies in flying ships, bringing gifts, during World War II; and still try to entice the gods back by making primitive models of planes, airstrips, and hangars to the stone carvings on 'ancient' Balinese temples showing Dutchmen sometimes riding in automobiles and sometimes belaboring the natives (at a time when it was still feasible to belabor the indigenous population).

There is nonetheless, a frequently recurrent theme concerning air travel in ancient myths and tradition, such as Icarus, the Cretan of the waxed wings who, according to legend, flew too close to the sun; Elijah and his fiery chariot; Endiku the Babylonian who was carried heavenwards and reported, rather aptly from our space travel viewpoint, that the land resembled porridge and the sea, a water trough; and the landing from the sky by the goddess Orejona (or Orellana) in Tiahuanaco; and frequent references to flying chariots in the Indian *Mahabharata*. All of these cases prove only that people had often considered travel by air a possibility in past eons. There is, however, a very tantalizing set of instructions in the Indian *Samarangana Sutradhara* of how, in effect, to build your own *vimana*, as these Hindu flying chariots were called. These do-it-yourself instructions contained some rather surprising detail:

... Strong and durable must the body be made, like a great flying bird, of light material. Inside it one must place the Mercury-engine with its iron heating apparatus beneath. By means of the power latent in the mercury which sets the driving whirlwind in motion, a man sitting inside may travel a great distance in the sky in a most marvellous manner.

Similarly by using the prescribed processes one can

39

build a Vimana as large as the temple of the God-in-motion. Four strong mercury containers must be built into the interior structure. When these have been heated by controlled fire from the iron containers, the vimana develops thunder-power through the mercury. And at once it becomes like a pearl in the sky.

Moreover, if this iron engine with properly welded joints be filled with mercury, and the fire be conducted to the upper part, it develops power with the roar of a lion ...

A more precise indication of the hitherto unsuspected mechanical advancement of the far past has come to us from the sea bottom of the Aegean, where it had lain for about 2000 years and then lay still another half-century in a museum before it was finally recognized for what is was—a computer for the stars.

The sea, especially the clear inner seas like the Mediterranean and Aegean, have proved to be a sort of archaeological storehouse, since most of that which has fallen, sunk, or been thrown into it since ancient times is still there. Off the island of Antikythera, in 1900, Greek sponge divers discovered a marvelous sunken cargo of Greek statues, perhaps loot from Greece en route to Rome.

Among the bronze statues subsequently brought up with difficulty by 'hard-hat' divers working at considerable depths at the cost of several fatalities, were some pieces of bronze and wood stuck or fused together. It was thought to be unidentified pieces of a statue or even, because of something that seemed to be wheels, a child's toy. These were put aside to see where they 'fitted.' As it turned out, they did not fit anywhere but were in themselves a more remarkable find than the beautiful statues. For when the wood dried a geared mechanism appeared, with inscriptions and directional indications, which when they could be interpreted revealed some startling information.

The secret took some years to unravel, through the work of many archaeologists, from Professor Stais, who first realized

40

its implications, to Dean Merritt, who dated the style of letters as the first century B.C., to Derek de Solla Price and George Stamires, whose research on the dials and mechanisms established its use and identity.

An elaborate system of gears, plates, and dials enabled the use of the machine to have at hand a miniature planetarium, mechanically supplying information regarding the phases, risings and settings of the moon, planets and the zodiacal constellations and other bright stars, working along the principles of a very complicated and ingenious clock. The meshing of the different sets of gears imply a differential gear system. In the words of Professor Price: 'Nothing like this instrument is preserved elsewhere. Nothing comparable to it is known from any scientific text or literary allusion.'

A further cogent point made by Price is that this or like models may have been the ancestor of the modern planetarium as well as of mechanical clocks. An unusual fact about clocks is that the first ones, from the Middle Ages, were the most complicated and comprehensive, and seemingly more concerned with phases of the moon and the planets than with telling time, the latter function being a logical development of the former.

Dr. Price notes the similarity to geared calendar computers of later Arabic civilization and observed: 'It seems likely that the Antikythera tradition was part of a large corpus of knowledge that has since been lost to us but was known to the Arabs ... developed and transmitted by them to medieval Europe, where it became the foundation for the whole range of subsequent invention in the field of clockwork ...'

Additional material from the Antikythera find lies on the bottom, too deep at present, successfully to salvage. But the world's ocean and sea bottoms are full of promise for the archaeologist. For the sea, 'the wine dark road' of Homer, was a road indeed, the great highway of antiquity. Other even more unusual finds are likely to be made on the continental shelves and the sea bottom itself, not only statues and other artifacts but whole cities and eventually, perhaps, clues to a civilization that preceded the ones of which we are aware.

CHAPTER THREE

THE LOST KNOWLEDGE OF HISTORY

It has been calculated that considerably less than 10 percent of the records of antiquity have come down to us. When one considers, however, the difficulties of preserving such records, and the vicissitudes through which they have passed, it is a wonder that we have even as much as we do. Much of the recorded material we do have has reached our present age because it was cut on stone, painted or incised on tomb walls, baked in clay tablets, or incribed on seals. Such material is often of a laudatory or commemorative nature and is rarely the literary or social commentary material which would give us a better insight on how the past really was, which we often are able to get from other unexpected sources.

Much of the ancient literature that could have come down to us has been destroyed by fire, either intentionally or by chance. Ancient 'books' were really long papyrus or parchment scrolls kept in libraries in certain of the great metropoli or palace cities and which could be copied by hand for one's own library providing one had permission to do so and enough educated slave power to get the job done. This had the effect of limiting the number of editions of any original manuscript and made masterpieces more vulnerable to loss and destruction.

Many ancient libraries were destroyed by fire or pillage, including the destruction of Persepolis, the capital of the Persian Empire, burned when conquered by Alexander the Great; the destruction of Phoenician and Carthaginian books in the Library of Carthage by the Romans in 146 B.C. and the later sacks of Rome and other cities of the collapsing Roman Empire and the subsequent repeated pillagings of

Constantinople.

Tremendous loss of books by fire was inadvertently caused by Julius Caesar when he captured Alexandria, but Caesar, being an author himself, was quick to disclaim responsibility and blamed the holocaust of books on the Alexandrines for resisting him. The Library of Alexandria survived this destruction and became again a center of learning and the chief book repository of the Mediterranean world until Omar, the Third Caliph of Islam, caused its millions of book rolls to be used for heating the city's baths (they lasted six months), when his general, Amru, conquered Alexandria in A.D. 636. The caliph is reported to have decreed: 'The contents of these books are in conformity with the Koran or they are not. If they are, the Koran is sufficient without them; if they are not they are pernicious. Let them, therefore, be destroyed.'

Besides the burning of ancient records as the result of conquest, many were intentionally destroyed by overzealous early Christians, often under the express exhortations of their bishops, with a zeal and basic reasoning which they shared with Omar, although they predated him by several centuries.

Other more cogent reasons for the destruction of ancient written works included using them for writing new material, erasing, scratching out, or covering the original writing, especially in the early Middle Ages when new writing materials had grown increasingly scarce. Other manuscripts were even used in Egypt as part of mummy wrappings—a gruesome but oddly effective way of preserving some of these manuscripts.

Besides the destruction of ancient records in the Mediterranean world and the Middle East by the misfortunes of war, conquest, or fanaticism, we find in China history's outstanding case of a single individual expunging the written past to immortalize himself, when Shih Huang Ti, the unifying Emperor of the Chin Dynasty (which gave China our name for it), adopted the political and psychological concept that Chinese history should start with him. In the third century B.C. he decreed that all books should be burned (even including those of Confucius) and sent scholars slow to destroy them to the unscholarly and often fatal labour of building the Great

43

Wall. The emperor excepted only books dealing with medicine, agriculture, and necromancy. As Chinese civilization had given rise to eminent scientific advances in very early times we do not know what knowledge and what references may have been lost, although certain medical practices such as acupuncture—piercing the head, shoulders, and joints with long needles to restore the balance of yang-yin, the positive and negative forces in the body—dates from those very ancient times and is still used and encouraged by the present rulers of China.

The use of the compass may be an instance of scientific knowledge preserved as magic while its true purpose was forgotten and then once more recognized. Chinese necromancers used polished hermitite ladles, sometimes balanced, sometimes half floating, to tell fortunes, but these artifacts also served for establishing directions, both for ships and chariots, as the indicators pointed due north and due south, the south pole being regarded as the principal pole (perhaps a memory of former voyages?) by the ancient Chinese.

It is not completely clear whether the ancient Chinese developed explosives locally or preserved this knowledge from an earlier source, as seems to be the case of the ancient inhabitants of India. The use of explosives in the Far East appears much older than was previously supposed, and not as a diversion but as a weapon. Some sort of explosives were used against Alexander the Great by the Indians and explosive rockets were used by the Chinese against the Mongols and other Turkic invaders. In fact the only battle that dynastic China ever successfully fought against modern invaders was a defeat she inflicted on one of the earlier Russian probes to the East, almost 200 years ago, during the early days of her last dynasty. The Russians had guns, it is true, but although the Chinese had only bows, arrows, swords, and spears to oppose them, they also had offensive rockets.

According to recent reports, Chinese scholars are presently researching antique documents, not only for the purpose of filling in history, but to see what can be learned from them of scientific knowledge, written in more or less disguised terms as was customary in remote times, when handed down knowledge was purposely kept secret by those who controlled it. An analogous search of ancient Arabic records is taking place in Russia and Arab countries, as interesting information about rockets, explosives, and chemical reactions, inherited from earlier sources of antiquity by the great Moslem centres of Cordova, Granada, Cairo, and Baghdad may contain, like the map of Piri Reis, information indicative of the scientific advancement of the past and, in the case of the former, relevant to the probable development of the future.

Destruction of ancient records continued with the discovery and conquest of the New World when Bishop Diego de Landa in Yucatán, in the early sixteenth century, caused to be destroyed all the Maya chronicles he could find (written on bark paper they burned nicely) and thereby probably destroyed any possible key for reading the hieroglyphics carved on stone or the three books which survived the burning—whose number tentatively rose to four in 1971 when another appeared from 'confidential' sources.

It should be noted that Bishop de Landa eventually became interested in the very material he had destroyed and, in a confused muddle of archaeological research, invented an imaginary alphabet by interviewing surviving Mayas, who nervously told him whatever they thought he wanted to hear. (The Maya system of writing consisted of hieroglyphics, of which even today we can identify only a few, and were not letters at all.) This Maya 'alphabet' which never existed has survived to contribute considerable confusion to some researchers of the nineteenth century, as in the case where this imaginary alphabet of de Landa was used by two French scholars to 'translate' a part of a surviving Maya 'book'—the *Codex Troano*. Both Brasseur de Bourbourg and Auguste Le Plongeon thought that the passage they studied described the sinking of the 'Land of Clay Hills, Mu ... in the ocean, together with its 64,000,000 inhabitants ... 8060 years ago ...'—calling to mind the phrase historian Robert Silverberg applied to a similar instance ... '[it] has about it the fascination of lunacy, like some monstrous bridge constructed of toothpicks ...'

Considering that there is such a small percentage of ancient knowledge that we can examine, and much that we cannot correctly read, or that we can read but which has been copied and recopied from ancient records often with errors and omissions (the sea maps of antiquity seem to have become less exact the more they were copied) we still detect a mysterious and inexplicable feature running through such scientific knowledge of the past as we have at our disposal.

There are strong indications that certain astronomical and scientific knowledge was known in the far past when, according to what we judge to be the technical capacity of the era, there was no way of making the necessary observations for such discovery. Even more so since much of this knowledge seems to come from an extremely early stage of development or to have been known by races and nations from their earliest culture periods, as if they had possessed this knowledge when their own culture began, instead of having slowly developed it.

There are clear indications that the Babylonians and other early peoples knew a great deal more about astronomy than did the races that came after them in all the centuries between the far past and the Renaissance. Some of this knowledge was early acquired or inherited and was passed down, often as legend, cropping up again and again in unexpected places at time spots when such information should not logically be known. Specifically it is considered unlikely that the Babylonians used fairly modern telescopes, yet without the use of telescopes they could not have seen, recorded, and passed on some of the astronomical features they observed.

Pioneers in the study of the early civilization of Mesopotamia, such as Rawlinson, were surprised to discover that the Babylonians knew certain unexpected details about the planets. Rawlinson suspected '... distinct evidence that they observed the four satellites of Jupiter and strong reason to believe that they were acquainted ... with the seven satellites of Saturn ...'

Babylonian books, in the shape of cuneiform writing on

baked clay cylinders, tell us of the 'horns of Venus,' which we describe as the 'phases' of Venus—not discernible without the use of a telescope. The constellation which we still call Scorpio as it was called in ancient times, does not look especially like a scorpion but did resemble one when one could see, with a telescope, a comet within it, forming the scorpion's 'tail.' Oddly enough, the scorpion was also called by the Maya word for 'scorpion,' either meaning that it was a shared tradition or that the early Mayas has some means of discerning the comet tail from their solidly built and exactly oriented jungle observatories.

Acquired scientific knowledge can take the form of legend as it is passed down through the ages. The Babylonians and their predecessors, the Sumerians, as well as more ancient races, observed the shape and monthly recurrence of the zodiacal constellations and gave them the names of people, things, or animals which are even today increasingly important to a large segment of the population.

Clay tablets from Mesopotamia still survive in great quantities throughout the world. Some of them were destroyed by the fires of conquest while others were simply baked harder, outlasting the cities and cultures which produced them. Part of the royal library of Ashurbanipal, the Assyrian Emperor, reposes in the British Museum. This same book-collecting emperor is reported to have once told a group of scholars: 'There—in the desert—long ago there were mighty cities whose very walls have disappeared, but we still have records of their languages on our tablets ...'

Many of the tablets from the library of the emperor's palace at Nineveh have not been translated, partially because of the dearth of qualified translators and partially because much of the translated material seems to deal with mathematics or astrology. We may speculate on what unsuspected information is still concealed in the cuneiform letters of the untranslated clay tablets.

In effect, there is no reason to minimize them because of an emphasis on astrology since astrology, which means 'knowledge of the stars,' and astronomy, 'law of the stars,' were, to the ancient inhabitants of Mesopotamia, essentially the same science.

It was perhaps in the clear skies of the desert night that man first began to plot the course and influence of the moon, stars, and planets, a science which suggested and eventually brought about the systemization of counting, telling time, establishment of the calendar, writing, and advanced mathematics.

A Babylonian book on astronomy tells us that 'stars take the form of animals' better to remember and identify them, and, as the culture retrogresses, they *become* animals, heroes, or gods.

A legend current in antiquity spoke of Uranus eating and subsequently disgorging his children. This grisly legend disguised a scientific observation for, when modern telescopes were invented, we learned that Uranus did indeed regularly cover its moons which then became visible again when they came around its other side. But someone, somehow, had observed it thousands of years ago with some form of viewing apparatus of sufficient strength to enable them to see and record it.

It occurred to several writers at the general time of the re-birth of knowledge, the Renaissance, to wonder how and where the ancients had received their scientific information. Sir Walter Raleigh, the explorer, seafarer, and scientist, wondered editorially, in a book on world history he finished in 1616, how ancient authors had known about the phases of Venus, which had only recently been discovered by Galileo.

As a further and striking instance of anachronism, Jonathan Swift, writing *Gulliver's Travels* in 1726 inexplicably describes the 'stars' or 'satellites' of Mars, which were not discovered until 1877. He even gives their measurements:
'... Certain astrologers ... have likewise discovered two lesser stars or satellites, which revolve about Mars, whereof the innermost is distant from the centre of the primary planet exactly three of its diameters, and the outermost five; the former revolves in the space of ten hours, and the latter in twenty-one and a half ... which evidently shews them to be

governed by the same law of gravitation, that influences the other heavenly bodies.'

In his controversial book *Worlds in Collision* Professor Immanuel Velikovsky points out the approximate correctness of the information so informally given in *Gulliver's Travels*, a guess that was probably not a guess at all but a legend or tradition from a lost corpus of scientific knowledge.

Thales of Miletus, a Greek scientist and astronomer who is also credited with the invention of steampower, was reported by Herodotus to have successfully predicted an eclipse of the sun prior to its actual occurrence on May 25, 585 B.C. To predict an eclipse, however, three checking points at 120° longitude distant from each other must previously be established. Considering the limited picture of the known world that we believe existed at the time of Thales's prediction, what were Thales's check points and by what means did they communicate information to him?

A puzzling reference by Dante in his *Divine Comedy* suggests that he knew or had heard about the existence of the Southern Cross long before the voyages of exploration made European seamen familiar with this phenomenon visible only when one has passed the equator. In Purgatory of the *Divine Comedy* we find the following six lines:

> *Io mi volsi a man destra e posi mente*
> *All'altro polo, e vidi quattro stelle*
> *Non viste mai fuor ch'alla prima gente.*

> *Goder parea il ciel lor fiammelle:*
> *O settentrional vedovo sito*
> *Poi che privato sei di veder quelle!*

> *(I turned to the right hand and looked toward*
> *The other pole, and I saw four stars,*
> *Never before seen except by the first people.*

> *The sky appeared to sparkle with their flames:*
> *O widowed northern land*
> *To be deprived of seeing them!)*

This allusion is myterious for more reasons than the references to an unknown phenomenon and the 'first people.' One wonders why Dante took the trouble to incorporate this astronomical observation in his masterpiece unless perhaps such fragments of ancient knowledge were relatively familiar to the educated elite who were his public. It is also true that many thousands of years ago the Southern Cross was visible in the Northern Hemisphere. Did Dante know this? And, if he did, as his reference 'never before seen except by the first people' would indicate, how did he know it was still visible in the Southern Hemisphere?

Ancient writers such as Homer and Virgil considered the red planet as Mars, the God of War, and specifically pointed out that *two* steeds drew his chariot through the heavens, giving them the names of 'Phobos' (Terror) and 'Deimos' (Rout)—a literary example of expressing knowledge through legend. When Asaph Hall finally discovered the moons of Mars in 1877 he fittingly named them after the turbulent horses of the God of War, a graceful gesture from the comparative present to the continuum of knowledge from the past, half lost but eventually reaffirmed.

Far back in the beginnings of world history we find an inexplicable preoccupation with mathematics and an ability to calculate enormous sums that were later neglected in the classical periods with which we are more familiar, such as the Greek and Roman cultures. The Greeks, although we trace back to them our own concept of geometry and trigonometry through Pythagoras, Euclid, Hippocrates, and others (although it is probable that they inherited knowledge from dynastic Egypt where builders had long known the square of the hypotenuse and other geometric data) were not interested in the calculation of enormous mathematical sums. As far as the Romans and mathematics are concerned it is noteworthy that a theory exists that one of the multiple reasons for the decline and fall of Rome was that the relatively clumsy Roman system of counting and calculating broke down when dealing with the increasing demands for calculation of money, goods, population, and trade in the enormous empire. The Romans did not use zero although its concept existed many centuries before them and, without zero, involved calculations are difficult, to say the least.

The Babylonians, who were able to resolve simultaneous equations, were familiar with the concept of zero and capable of dealing easily with enormous numbers—which we would write using 15 or 20 ciphers—using them to calculate dates and time periods on a cosmic scale. In addition to a system of 10s and multiplication by 20s the Babylonians or their predecessors gave us the 12 or 60 system, not only convenient for minutes, hours, months, and years, but of greater use than the decimal system for calculating division, since 12 divides into more numbers than 10.

The importance of the number 12 was very probably suggested to the prehistoric astronomers by the recurring procession of the 12 zodiacal constellations, and the realization of the importance and extraordinary utility of the number, inspired from what they observed from the night skies, must have given the first astronomers a feeling of having received a message from the gods.

For the purpose of advanced mathematics, zero is the secret ingredient. Very ancient cultures knew about it and often, as cultural decadence occurred, they forgot it. The Babylonians used the concept, writing it by a blank space (a rather apt way to express 'nothing'), but its use eventually disappeared, a retrograde phenomenon which occurred in China as well. Ancient India, reputed to have 'invented' it, knew it and kept it until, through the Arabs, it was brought again to the Middle East and finally to Europe.

But on exactly the opposite side of the world from India we find the zero in use in the Maya cities and observatories for thousands of years. The Mayas were perhaps the outstanding astronomers of pre-Columbian America, although all the settled tribes and nations seemed preoccupied with the study of the heavens. The Mayas, or perhaps their predecessors, the Olmecs, came closest of all ancient peoples to calculating the exact length of the solar year, a measurement known to our own civilization only comparatively recently. The true

51

measurement of the solar year is 365.2422 days, and the Mayas, through techniques and calculations not yet fully understood, were able to come as close as 365.2420 days, an almost negligible difference.

What may be an equally remarkable astronomical achievement is the solid 10-ton gate standing on a 13,000-foot plateau at Tiahuanaco, Bolivia, a solitary doorway leading to no evident place. Carved on it is a system of designs thought to deal

The Gate of the Sun, Tiahuanaco, Bolivia, inexplicably cut from a single piece of stone and weighing over ten tons.

with the position of the moon according to the time of day and indications regarding the equinoxes and solstices. The moon's real and apparent movements are indicated, showing an awareness on the part of the original carvers, of the rotation of the earth. The age of Tiahuanaco has not been established, even the Aymará Indians found there by the Spanish conquerors did not know who had built the enormous doorway —other than the gods.

The approximately round shape of the earth was generally known and accepted in remote periods of civilization and in far corners of the earth. An early Hindu work, the *Surya Siddhanta*, describes the earth as a planet with overtones of relativity:

> ...Everywhere on the sphere men think their own place to be on top. But since it is a sphere in the void, why should there be an above and an underneath?

Ancient records in India show a familiarity with most parts of the world, even including such exotic and distant places as Ireland.

Children in ancient Egypt, according to hieroglyphic inscriptions at Sakkara, were taught that the world was round. The Greek scientist Eratosthenes, in the third century B.C. measuring the angle of the sun at noon in Syene and in Alexandria, estimated the circumference of the earth, missing it by only a few hundred miles. Most of the measurements of the ancient sea maps could have been made only with cognizance of the roundness of the world.

There is even what may be a reference to the American continent in Plato's dialogue of *Timaeus*. Critias, one of the speakers in this dialogue, written about 2400 years ago is setting the stage for a description of Atlantis but in doing so he makes an unusually intriguing comment which may refer to America. He says:

> ... in those days the Atlantic was navigable; and there was an island situated in front of the straits which you call the Columns of Heracles: the island was larger than Libya and Asia put together, and was the way to other islands, and from the islands you might pass through the whole of the opposite continent which surrounded the true ocean; for this sea which is without the Straits of Heracles is only a harbour, having a narrow entrance, but that other is a real sea, and the surrounding land may be most truly called a continent...

Plato's references to the sunken continent of Atlantis are

still a fascinating subject for study and speculation, but his reference to a continent on the other side of the 'true ocean' is a reality, a fact that he had heard or known of 2000 years before Columbus.

Columbus was so fascinated by the second act of Seneca's *Medea*, written about 1500 years before his time, that he copied it out in longhand and often referred to it. Although Seneca in his *Medea* is not so explicit as Plato, the excerpt is equally thought provoking. The Latin version, as Columbus read it, is followed by an approximate literal translation:

> *Venient annis saecula seris*
> *Quibus oceanus vincula rerum*
> *Laxet et ingens pateat tellus*
> *Tethisque novos detegat orbes*
> *Nec sit terris ultima Thule.*

(... There will come centuries in the late ages of the world
During which the ocean, the fetters of things
Will relax; and the world will appear vast
And The Sea will reveal new continents
And Thule will no longer be the end of the world ...)

The suggestion of unknown continents or land existing beyond where the world was supposed to end was a source of inspiration to Columbus who researched his projected voyage with praiseworthy and understandable zeal and collected many classical allusions and theories concerning the true shape of the world.

Naturally not all the Greeks or Romans of antiquity believed in the flatness of the earth, in Apollo and his sun chariot, the entrances to Hades at certain definite locations and other pleasant fancies relative to the cosmos, nor did reflective Hindus believe that a flat world was supported by four giant elephants standing on the back of an even more gigantic tortoise, any more than Americans believe in the actual existence of Santa Claus, comic strip characters, or the Easter or Playboy bunny. However, when a documented 'intuition' or 'guess' made long before their discovery, indicated the existence of moons around Jupiter, Uranus, and the rings of Saturn, the dimensions of the moons of Mars, a description of the Southern Cross, and the presence of a transoceanic continent with its adjacent islands, we get the distinct impression that someone traveled this way before us.

While these astronomical and geographical 'previews' which we find in ancient records indicate a literary retention of a wider and older knowledge, certain mechanical artifacts of which we have pictorial representations or reports give an oddly modern aspect to the past.

Napalm, for example, strikes an extremely current note but the 'Greek fire' employed by the warships of ancient Byzantium, manufactured by a special formula including naphtha and sulphur or petroleum and saltpeter, had somewhat the same effect as napalm and, impervious to water, would keep on burning when water was thrown upon it and even burn on the sea into which the survivors of a burning enemy ship would jump. Stoppered jars of this chemical warfare weapon were self-igniting and could either be hurled from catapults, fired by means of rockets, or pumped through a bronze-lined flame thrower at the enemy ships. Byzantine marines were often equipped with portable flame throwers, so small that they could be carried like a pistol.

The extraordinary inventions of Archimedes of Syracuse, (287–212 B.C.), some of which may have resulted from the time he spent as a student at the Library of Alexandria, encompassed a revised version of the screw pump, ingenious systems of levers, pulleys, and grips for lifting great weights, one use of which was to grab besieging Roman war galleys in the harbour of Syracuse and tilt and sink them, and a method of refraction of solar rays to set ships afire.

Modern 'improvements' as seen in antiquity were not always war-connected. The palace culture of Crete (2500 B.C.) featured running water, flushing toilets in beautiful apartments with walls decorated with frescoes of dolphins and nude girls jumping over enormous bulls in early versions of the bullfight. Babylonian business tycoons dictated letters to secretaries who inscribed them on clay tablets in their offices in enormous brick emporia. The clay envelopes containing these letters have occasionally been found unopened with the business letters still inside. Hot water on tap was available from boilers in ancient Rome and thermos containers, which kept foods and liquids either hot or cold, were in common use. Time was calculated in a fairly accurate manner by water clocks, based on 12, not 24, divisions of the day and night. Enormous stone blocks were lifted onto buildings by huge cranes whose motive power was furnished by a few slaves walking on connected treadmills.

Medical and surgical techniques were not surpassed or even caught up with until the nineteenth century and some brain surgery, accomplished in ancient Egypt, has not yet been clearly understood or duplicated. Other random bits of what may be traceable to ancient attainments in medicine may have survived through the Middle Ages disguised in the nostrums of witchcraft and magic as, for example, the use of spider webs (penicillin) for treatment of wound infections. Records from ancient India, thousands of years old, deal with plastic surgery, brain and Caesarean section operations, and herbal treatments for rejuvenation of vitality, memory, teeth, eyesight, and skin tone—a subject of no less interest today than in ancient times.

In the last two centuries B.C. the Library of Alexandria became a principal research centre of the classical world. Hero, a Greek scientist, compiled a study of engineering techniques and developed a 'machine tool,' that is, a tool for cutting screws and a steam turbine using steam for the first *recorded* time as a source of power. However, in a world where slave power was inexhaustible, this latter use was not then exploited.

The great Archimedes, who also did extensive research in Alexandria, is credited with having invented the Archimedes screw although there are indications that this invention was used in Egypt centuries before and was part of the general stockpile of knowledge there available.

Ctesibius, another Alexandrine scholar, developed a fire engine with a double action pump, an especially useful apparatus in cities where landlord tactics often forced overcrowding in huge firetrap multiple dwelling buildings, again a curiously modern note, which was partially rectified in Rome by prohibiting 'high rise' constructions of such residences.

Romans of the Western and Eastern Empires had indirect interior lighting; 'unbreakable' walls and floors of glass; a system of radiant heat and even oil heat (in Byzantium) for the great baths. The Roman aqueduct water system with its structured plan of valves and pumps, so solidly built that it is still in use, could supply water so quickly that the whole arena could be filled to a depth sufficient to float ships for naval battles during short intermissions between other entertainments.

Just before the time that the Roman Empire fell apart and Europe retrogressed into semi-barbarism, 'modernization' had reached such a stage that even multiple harvesters were used in reaping grain, perhaps an instance of forced inventiveness as the slave population ran low. Features like this have not been mentioned in surviving annals, perhaps not even considered worthy of mention, and would not even be suspected if a sculptured block showing a multiple reaper had not been discovered among Roman remains in France several years ago.

Apart from these modern features of ancient cultures certain techniques suggest that antiquity may have developed some processes that we have not yet discovered. We know, for example, that iron and steel rust, when exposed to the elements, within a relatively short time. We know that the ancient Egyptians possessed iron but never found any to have survived until the opening of the unrobbed royal tomb of the Pharaoh Tut-ankh-amen.

An unusual example of unrusting iron, however, has apparently been standing out in the elements for more than a thousand years with no ill effects.

In a courtyard of the Qutb Minar in Delhi, India, stands the Ashoka Pillar, a column of cast iron about 30 feet high which was torn from its setting at Muttra and transported to

Delhi by the Moslem invaders of India in the tenth century. Prior to this it had stood in its temple at Muttra for more than six hundred years, where it was topped by a Garuda, the bird shape assumed by the god Vishnu during one of his periodic savings of humanity. The Garuda, as well as the other columns, if there were any, has long since disappeared, possibly smelted into the swords of Moslem conquerors. A most unusual aspect of the surviving column is the fact that it should not be there at all as both iron and steel rust over a period of years and certainly would have rusted away over a period of sixteen or more centuries. The possible use of some metallurgical secret ingredient or process being used may well be the explanation of its longevity and is yet another reminder of ancient techniques being lost or forgotten with the passing of time.

Although the planetary bodies have been given the names of mythological gods or heroes (which we still use) there seems to have been considerable former observation of them more concerned with science than mythology. We suspect, because of ancient knowledge of and reference to heavenly bodies not visible to the naked eye, that some sort of telescope was once known and then forgotten. Plutarch attributes the use of optical instruments to Archimedes who used them '... to manifest ... the largeness of the sun.' But although we have found no such instruments dating from ancient times, we do have at hand what may be smaller examples proving ancient use of magnification.

As long ago as 1853 an object was presented at the British Association for the Advancement of Science by a Sir David Brewster. The object was an optical lens, a perfect lens according to the standards of the day. What was unusual about this particular lens was that it had been excavated in the ruins of Nineveh, capital of the Assyrian Empire, and was found in ruins dated about 600 B.C. As far as anyone knew, ground lenses were not known until nineteen centuries later. Although its authenticity was not attacked at the time, its use was strongly questioned and it was judged to be a jewel or other decoration and, although coincidentally a lens, was not used as one by the ancient Assyrians. The presence of an optical lens, under other strata in the ruins of Nineveh, was considered simply to be without explanation and the lens, jewel, decoration, or whatever it was, ended up in the British Museum.

Since then, other ancient lenses have been found in different parts of the world including Lybia, Iraq, Mexico, Ecuador, and even Central Australia. A concave ground obsidian lens was brought up from the sea bottom at Esmeraldas, Ecuador, and minuscule concave mirrors, ground by an unknown process, and which may have been used for magnification, have been unearthed at La Venta, Mexico, attributed to the Olmec culture, presently thought to be the most ancient in Mexico.

Some technical aid of this sort may provide an explanation of the metal and semiprecious stone working technique of the pre-Columbian American cultures. Hyatt Verrill has commented on the mystery of '... How ancient civilized races of America performed their amazing feats and accomplished such astonishing works in metals and the hardest of stones. How they fashioned minute, chased gold beads—often built up of several pieces—no larger than the head of a pin; how they cut, polished, perforated and carved topaz, amethyst, garnet, agate, crystal and other precious stones; how they worked friable obsidian into thin polished rings...'

It is notable, however, that the Amerindian cultures reached a plateau of civilization long before the conquest of America; it almost seems that, from comparative barbarism, they started at the plateau.

An outstanding example of lost knowledge suggests itself concerning the knowledge or lack of knowledge of the wheel. It is well known that when the first Spanish conquerors came to the American mainland and first encountered the advanced Indian culture of Mexico, Central America, and the Andean Plateau—they found remarkable paved roads, passages over and tunnels through mountains, causeways over lakes and long suspension bridges—in a word, everything necessary for a highly developed transportation system except the logical means of transportation—wagons, carts, or chariots. But there were no wheels; everything was transported by safari-like human caravans or, in the Andes, on the backs of llamas as well as human beings. In Inca times, human runners (*chasquis*) became almost a selective breed, being able to cover ground so quickly in relays that the Inca, in his mountain capital, received and ate fresh fish from the coast, fresher, be it said in passing, than the fish now available in Cuzco, the former Inca capital. But in spite of all the organization, building culture, technical advancement, transportation of goods and food in the Indian empires, the lack of wheels has usually been accepted as proof that the pre-Columbian inhabitants of America had never graduated from the Stone Age.

One developing disadvantage to this generally held theory is that wheels keep turning up in connection with ancient Mexican artifacts—usually in the form of models or wheeled toys representing dogs (or coyotes) and carts. The wheels have been found at different sites in Mexico—Cholula, Oaxaca, Tres Zapotes, and El Tajín, near Vera Cruz, and in

Pre-Columbian wheeled dog excavated near Vera Cruz, Mexico. Wheels of any sort had long been thought to be unknown to pre-Columbian Amerinds but increasing numbers of wheeled toys (if they were toys) have been found.

the Republic of Panama. It seems unlikely that the ancient Americans would 'invent' wheels for toys and not for more important uses nor can we be sure that the circular disks we see on pre-Columbian monuments are not derivations or predecessors of the wheel. We cannot even be sure that what look like toys *are* toys; artifacts may have had different uses and meanings from those that we, from a point of view alien in time and culture, apply to them.

For example, one wonders what could be the meaning of

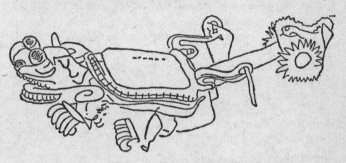

Side view of pre-Columbian golden jaguar figure found in Coclé, Panama, which has been suggested to be a stylized model of an ancient geared earth-moving machine. (From drawing by Ivan Sanderson)

an extraordinary gold and jeweled model of what appears to be either a long jaguar or a short crocodile, excavated from pre-Columbian graves of the little known Coclé culture of Panama by museum and university expeditions in the 1920s, now on view in the University of Pennsylvania in Philadelphia. The unusual feature of the artifact is that it contains cogwheels on an axle with a rocker arm between them with two more rocker arms in the rear and the mouth of the jaguar has teeth like bucket grabs. Dr. Ivan Sanderson, who has examined the object in detail and who is also familiar with live jaguars (and crocodiles), is of the opinion that it is a model of a form of pre-Columbian earth mover or bulldozer constructed in the form of a modified jaguar. He also ob-

61

serves: 'the joints of the legs are hinged the wrong way for an animal but the right way for heavy-duty shock absorbers.' As this unusual artifact is uncomplete, we can only wonder whether it was a prehistoric model of a real working vehicle, which would explain some of the construction triumphs of the pre-Columbians, or whether it was simply a geared child's toy, like the dogs with wheels, in a land where the principle of the wheel was supposed to be unknown.

There are many such anomalies among the great pre-Columbian cultures destroyed by the Spaniards as well as

Top view of golden jaguar, showing spade-like features on side and in rear. Dotted lines on right side show probable matching attachment, since disappeared. Lower right shows sketch of modern earth mover for purpose of comparison. (From drawings by Ivan Sanderson)

among the races that had preceded them and had already disappeared or been destroyed at the time of the Conquest. We do not know, for example, how the ancient Peruvians were able to move enormous monoliths and fit them so exactly together with the tools they had at hand, nor how they were able to perform delicate operations of trepanning, the removal of a section of the skull and the insertion of a gold or copper plate, a form of brain surgery, as well as other delicate operations concerned with filling and capping teeth, or the system of medicine which led to the development of drugs at an early period, or how the Colombian Chibchas and the Peruvian Chimús plated precious metals without the use of electricity. We do not even know the use of many of the artifacts still existing—as to why, for example, there are carved stone chairs in uncounted numbers scattered through the highlands of Colombia without nearby vestiges of buildings, or whether some of the laboriously modified hillsides and mountaintops were made for amphitheaters as well as for irrigation purposes. There must have been a reason for the profusion of giant round stone balls on the west coast of Mexico and Costa Rica, but it is unknown to us.

We do not even know the true names of many of the vanished Amerindian cultures, but simply ascribe to them the names of present places where their remains have been found. Some of these Amerindian origins might be clarified if we could read, or even find, any indigenous records, although the many surviving Maya inscriptions, plentifully at hand in the Yucatán Peninsula and Central America, are still largely a mystery to us, except for numbers and dates. Russian anthropologists and archaeologists have applied modern methods of computerization to this ancient script at the Computer Centre of Novosibersk, but while they have so far produced interesting and well documented reports on the methods used (in three volumes), they have not yet 'broken' the script, if indeed it is a script. It now appears that a thousand combinations or separate constituents have been identified in Maya writing, consisting of one-part, two-part, or three-part glyphs and their combinations. We do not know, however, whether the Mayan language spoken today in its different dialects is indeed the language of the Maya glyphs. These fascinating signs may remain a mystery unless, as has been suggested, some lost remnant of surviving Mayas of the ancient culture still living in the jungle might someday be located who had preserved the secret of the script. One such bona fide refugee group, the Lacandón Indians of the Chiapas rain forest, who fled the Spaniards hundreds of years ago, and who have been much researched in recent years, had preserved certain Maya traditions but had apparently forgotten any knowledge of writing.

In South America there exist written inscriptions, located in various places of the Andean Plateau and the Amazon River system, often untranslatable and unidentifiable, as well as an odd legend from Inca times telling that writing was once known in Peru and adjoining lands, but was abolished under pain of death by an ancient ruler who had been advised by the priests that it was the cause of a plague then besetting his empire (one might almost presume an allegorical allusion to the power of the written word). Except for these vague and unproved indications, however, no datable written or carved inscriptions have been found from the prehistoric empires of South America.

The Empire of the Incas, however, employed an unusual substitute for writing, the use of which has perhaps not yet been fully understood. This was the *quipu*, a tasseled bundle of different colored knotted cords which the Spaniards saw in use throughout the Incaic Empire for the purpose of making reports on population, produce, tribute, military levies and apparently all the 'paper work' of the extremely well organized and essentially socialistic empire of the Incas. A special caste of *quipu* 'readers' was trained and kept at hand to translate these bundles of cords which kept such exact records that, it was said, if a sandal were missing in any part of the extensive empire the Inca would know about it. It may be, however, that the system of *quipus* was either a form of writing or even writing beyond writing, having somehow skipped the alphabet and gone into a system of computerization. When we consider the possible variants of separate elements in these implied memory banks in a *quipu* bundle, we must take into account not only the number of strings, their length, the color of the threads, the varying weaves, the frequency and spacing of the knots and even the form of each knot, the combinations are infinite and even the relaying of spoken words falls within the realm of possibility.

In assessing the scientific and mechanistic progress of ancient civilization throughout the world, apart from inventions relative to communication and records, relatively advanced techniques of building, mathematics, and medicine, scientific observance of visible nature and an idea of the world and the cosmos, one wonders whether the very ancient cultures of the world had any concept of atomic structure, the supreme and potentially final achievement of modern man.

In this regard there exist obscure though fascinating suggestions that several cultures, at some past period, knew about the composition of matter. Our own word 'atom' comes from the Greek construction meaning 'that which cannot be divided' or 'cut up.' There is even a reference in Democritus, however, attributed to Phoenician sources, that the indivisible atom was, in effect, divisible. Some of the Vedic and Buddhist texts of ancient India, moreover, contain descriptions of linkages of particles of entity which we can now understand in terms of the atomic theory and molecular interrelation although before access or reaccess to this knowledge these passages sounded like pure mystification.

Early Buddhist commentaries furnish easy to understand descriptions of the interrelation of molecules when they speak of bundles of reeds interreacting and connecting with other bundles of reeds and the necessity of disassociating the connections to escape rebirth and the wheel of existence, which may be simply another instance of ancient knowledge reappearing through philosophy.

The Indian writer and yogi, Paramhansa Yogananda, pointed out in 1945 (Year 1 of the Atomic Era) that a system of Hindu Philosophy, the Vaisesika, is derived from the Sanskrit word *visesas*, which can be translated as 'atomic individuality.' According to preserved records in Sanskrit, an Indian named Aulukya, in the eighth century B.C., was expounding, in his own words, what clearly seems to be such unexpectedly modern scientific theory as the atomic nature of matter, the spatial expanses between atoms in their own systems, the relativity of time and space, the theory of cosmic rays, the kinetic nature of all energy, the law of gravitation as inherent in 'earth' atoms, heat being the cause of molecular change.

It would be surprising if all of this knowledge of extreme antiquity, which modern man started rediscovering in the Renaissance and which he is still discovering, were chance realizations by ancient astronomers, mathematicians, philosophers, and teachers. It would perhaps be more understandable if we considered this knowledge as a residual legacy from an older widespread culture, or system of cultures, of which only a part, like the unsubmerged one-tenth of an iceberg, has come down to or been recognized by modern man.

CHAPTER FOUR

A TIME CAPSULE 45 STORIES HIGH

In addition to the many references to and hints of a former advanced culture and some inexplicable artifacts which may be vestiges of it, there may be one piece of prehistory civilization that has come down to us almost intact, so solid as to be almost indestructible, so familiar that its true message is obscure. This is the Great Pyramid of Gizeh, ascribed to the Pharaoh Khufu, the second Pharaoh of the IV Dynasty of Egypt and thought to have been constructed between 4500 and 5000 years ago. It is the biggest of the seventy pyramids of Egypt, and is even today, with some of the top removed, about 45 stories high, and composed of two and a half million blocks weighing $2\frac{1}{2}$ to 12 tons each.

But it is not for its height and mass that it is remarkable; it may have been, as well as a marker or prime meridian, an almost permanent time capsule of accumulated knowledge for an intervening period of history, between the end of an older culture and the start of a new one.

For although generations of tomb robbers and other seekers have searched for hidden treasure within the Great Pyramid, and the Arab rulers of Egypt in the Middle Ages tried to blast their way into its secret passages which have been located, lost and then found again in modern times, no great treasure, as far as we know, has been found, and in the 'King's Chamber' only an empty stone sarcophagus stands, with no evidence of prior vandalism or entry.

The greatest find, however, has been conveniently evident throughout all the centuries of our recorded history but was not recognized until modern knowledge 'caught up' with former knowledge and was able to recognize it. For the 'secret treasure' may have been its placement, its volume, its inner dimensions and even the direction of its inner passages.

Although it has been generally supposed that the Great Pyramid was built as a tomb for King Khufu there have been legends for its considerable life (or death) span of 4000 to 5000 or more years that there was a secret incorporated in this most famous of constructions. This tradition of secret wisdom was kept alive by the Copts, a native Christian sect who trace their ancestry back to the ancient Egyptians, as Egypt was Christianized several hundred years before the Moslem conquest, and who still today employ a church language related to or descended from ancient Egyptian and who have secret lodges where the gods of ancient Egypt are still held in honor.

A surviving Coptic text by Masudi, a Coptic writer of the Middle Ages, states in part:

Surid ... one of the Kings of Egypt before the Flood ... built two great pyramids ... He also ordered the priests to deposit therein the total of their wisdom and their knowledge of the different arts and sciences of mathematics and geometry so that they would be as a witness for the benefit of those who could eventually understand them...

The text continues, however, to deal with the pyramid and prophesy at which point the measurable or provable scientific investigation habitually breaks off and even directs a coldly reflective and doubting gaze back to what it has already been.

The Arabs, having conquered Egypt for Islam in the seventh century A.D., heard of the Coptic legends and of the treasure as well as manuscripts from 'before the Flood' stored there which contained all kinds of useful scientific knowledge, including secrets of immediate value concerning weapons that would not rust and glass that would not break. The reference to unbreakable glass occurs again and again in Arab legends of the secrets of antiquity—including the belief the celebrated Pharos of Alexandria, an estimated 600-foot-high lighthouse in front of the harbour, was set on solid blocks of glass.

Avid for the real or fancied treasure of the Great Pyramid, a Moslem Caliph of the Middle Ages, Al Mamun, ordered teams of workers to examine the north side looking for a secret entrance mentioned by the Roman writer Strabo, a search that was somewhat destructive as the caliph's engineers smashed and blasted their way into the pyramid, but definitely unrewarding. It did show, however, the existence of long passageways within the pyramid. Mamun's searchers followed other passages to the King's Chamber, where they found only an empty stone sarcophagus but no King Khufu and no treasure.

A realization of what may be the real secret of the Great Pyramid came about almost by chance at the beginning of the nineteenth century, during one of the many conquests of Egypt—this time by Napoleon and his army. When French Army engineers undertook to map Egypt they selected the Great Pyramid as a convenient point of triangulation.

When studying their triangulation points, they first noticed that the pyramid's east side pointed due east, aligned to the polar axis of the earth more correctly than could have possibly been done without modern instruments like the compass or even knowledge of the existence of the polar axis, previously thought to be a more or less 'modern' achievement. Subsequently it was discovered that if diagonal lines were extended from the southwest and southeast corners through the northeast and northwest corners these lines would conveniently and exactly enclose the Delta of the Nile, a welcome aid from the past for the purpose of surveying the area. Furthermore, the meridian passed through the apex of the pyramid, cutting the Nile Delta almost exactly in two. The exact position of the pyramid did not seem to be situated in any special relation to the Nile or to any particular spot *except* to coincide with the indicated measurements or boundaries they apparently delineated.

In fact the location of the pyramid would be, and probably was, an excellent place to establish a prime meridian, such as is presently the case with Greenwich since, if we follow the meridian which passes through the pyramid as it goes around the world, we find that it acts like a great dividing line separating the habitable continents into two equal parts and then, following it past the poles onto the other, or 'water,' side of the earth, it is again evident that it divides the Pacific into two fairly equal parts as well.

Herodotus, the Greek historian, and other ancient writers had reported that the exact slant height of the pyramid was a stadium long, that is, one six-hundredth of a degree of latitude. Agatharchides of Cnidus, writing in the second century B.C., reported that the length of a side of the great pyramid was one eighth of a minute of a degree of latitude.

These indications of geodesic measures, implying ancient knowledge of the dimensions of the earth, have long suggested that other measurements might be found if the pyramid were properly surveyed and examined. This has been the case for the past more than 200 years. It has been often and painstakingly measured by a whole series of archaeologists, scientists, surveyors, astronomers, cartographers, engineers, architects, astrologers, and mystics. Many of these scholars have devoted a large part of their lives and fortunes to the study and the interpretation of the 'secrets' of the pyramid.

In our day the base has been cleared for exact measurement and allowance has been made for the missing casing stones that once made the pyramid shine brightly in Egypt's sun before they were removed over the years for other buildings. Exact measurements of the inside and the outside of the pyramid has furnished us with a whole series of dimensions, the implications of which are almost as astonishing as the theory that the dimensions and turns of the pyramid's inner corridors and chambers record the past and foretell the future.

As the numerous theories regarding past and future history by measurement cannot be checked with any degree of accuracy and since the final predicted results are rather pessimistic (general world decline starts in 1962 and the 'calendar' comes to a stop in 2001), it is best to examine the coincidences in the form of the pyramid that are more subject to our control and appraisal.

But the interpretative results of measurements which we have at hand are astonishing enough. A few of the more readily understandable examples and statistics relatively easy to check give one the feeling that the Great Pyramid is indeed a library where huge and meticulously joined stones take the place of easily destroyed papyrus and parchment scrolls, a repository of scientific knowledge waiting in the desert like a gigantic time capsule only to be interpreted by future races with enough scientific preparation to do so.

The pyramid measurements apparently gives the *modern* value of *pi* as 3.1416, a figure obtained by dividing the sum distance of its sides by twice its height—a normal method of calculating the relation of a circumference to its radius. Previously, Greek mathematicians, including Archimedes, never got closer to the value of *pi* than 3.1428, and this, thousands of years after the pyramid was built. The 'pyramidal inch' is thought to be based on the actual size of the earth, as fifty such inches makes a length of almost exactly one ten-millionth of the polar axis.

With the scientific revolution which followed the French Revolution, French scientists adopted the meter as a unit of length, with no known reference to the pyramidal cubit, considering it to represent the one ten-millionth part of the meridian. In effect, however, it is short by one five-thousandth because the contours of the earth are not regular and each meridian has its own length. Therefore a more perfect unit would be one based not on the meridian but on the unchanging length of polar radius or axis, giving the end result that the Eyptian system was more logical than the present one.

With the establishment of the pyramidal inch an amazing series of coincidences falls into place: The sum of the base sides of the pyramid indicates the number of days in a year, or 365.240 pyramidal inches.

The height of the pyramid multiplied by ten million gives the approximate distance between the earth and the sun.

One pyramidal inch multiplied by 100,000,000 gives almost, but not quite, the distance covered by the earth in its orbit around the sun. The slight discrepancy, however, may be explained by the widening of the sun's orbit in 5000 or 6000 years.

By doubling the length of the four sides of the pyramid we get almost exactly the equivalent of one minute of a degree at the equator. (Measured in meters the pyramid figure is 1842.92 as against the present figure of 1842.78.)

The pyramid is so perfectly measured and built that if a radius is chosen equal to its height and used to draw a circle, the area of the circle drawn is equal to the square area of the base.

The earth's polar axis inclines to a different point in space each day and does not attain its original position except once in 25,827 years. This figure almost exactly occurs (25826.6) in pyramid measures by adding together the diagonal lines of the base of the pyramid.

The approximate weight of the pyramid is almost 600,000 tons. If we multiply it by one billion we get the approximate estimated weight of the earth.

An unusual indication of the age of the pyramid exists in its orientation to the North Star, clearly visible up through the millions of tons of perfectly set rock through the Grand Gallery which goes up to an opening at the upper side of the pyramid directly from the King's Chamber. Evidence has been offered that the North Star at the time it was 'captured' in the pyramid's sights was in the Dragon Constellation and has since become part of the Big Dipper, itself a part of the Great Bear.

This brings up the 'use' of the Great Pyramid—whether it had other uses than a tomb, a marker, a repository of knowledge and measures and an observatory. Apparently among its other uses, many of which are not yet clear, it was a tremendous seasonal clock and calendar. The slightly concave shape of the covering white limestone facing stones, since removed to build Cairo, made it possible for a shadow to be cast in varying lengths both of the pyramid and before it to indicate the arrival of the spring equinox, the passing of the year, and even the hours of the day.

Edmé François Jomard was a French pioneer in pyramidology whose interest in the Great Pyramid dated from the time of Napoleon's invasion of Egypt with his many divisions of soldiers and almost a division of scientists. Among his many contributions to the study of this phenomenon was his theory that the empty red granite sarcophagus in the King's Chamber was meant to be empty and perhaps was not a stone casket for a Pharaoh's mummy, but a container indicating a standard measure of volume, just as the pyramid itself seemed to be a measure of distances and other dimensions.

L. Sprague de Camp, a modern historian, writer, and archaeological investigator, expresses widespread scientific skepticism about considering everything in the pyramid a message when he comments concerning the empty stone casket:

> ... The sarcophagus was supposed to be a standard—as if anyone but a lunatic would take as a volumetric standard a vessel holding the awkward amount of a ton and a quarter of water and then shut it up in a man-made mountain so that it could not be used ...

Another like comment has been: '... the real mystery of the pyramid is that King Khufu changed his mind about being buried there,' since, as far as we know, the king's coffin has *always* been empty.

In accord with the proliferation of mysteries one encounters in the study of the Great Pyramid is the question of the other seventy-odd pyramids in Upper and Lower Egypt. Were they all tombs or did they mark something as well? Why, if they were the tombs of Pharaohs, are there more Pharaohs in history than there are pyramids? Take the case of the great Rameses II, whose self-adulation covered the walls of Egypt and who caused 65-foot-high statues of himself cut out of solid rock at Abu Simbel. (These statues were saved from flooding at the time of the construction of the Aswan Dam by cutting them from the rock and hoisting them to the top of the cliff, an operation financed largely by public contributions by individuals from nations Rameses never dreamed of, thousands of years after his death.) Where is the pyramid of this ancient master of public relations, as well as those of other great Pharaohs? Most probably the Pharaohs simply gave up the idea of being buried in pyramids as furnishing too signal a location for future tomb robbers.

There exists also the possibility that some of the other pyramids may be copies of the greatest one, without the builders understanding or caring to incorporate any messages other than a reminder of their personal fame. Herodotus relates a spicy tidbit of ancient gossip when he tells of an Egyptian princess, desirous of having her *own* pyramid, who sold herself to a vast succession of lovers in order to obtain the necessary construction funds—surely history's most original reason for a princess to become a prostitute.

In general, pyramids are considered, along with obelisks, to be related to sun worship, by marking the sun's progress in the day and year. 'Sun boats' for the buried Pharaohs to follow the sun into heaven have been found buried near some of the pyramids, exactly pointed on a west–east axis.

A most original theory was recently formulated (1971) by Dr. Kurt Mendelssohn of Oxford who offered the suggestion that the pyramids had been constructed to keep the large surplus labor force of Egypt busy during the annual three-month flood period of the Nile—in other words, that they were welfare work programs which would regulate work distribution by staggering the construction programs of successive pyramids and have the interesting side effect of unifying and controlling the economy of the country. We know from contemporaneous markings on pyramid stones that the workers, who were not slaves, were paid in wheat, beer, garlic, and other indispensables.

This theory may also apply in other sections of the world, such as the incredible roads and buildings of the 'socialistic' Inca Empire of South America, and the walls and canals of China, although it was not used by the Romans, who eventually fell under the weight of supporting their 'welfare' labor force. However, attributing modern theories and remedies to ancient cultures, whose real outlook we can only guess at, is hazardous at best. We can, for example, end up by equating the departure of the tribes of Israel from Egypt as a labor dispute over the amount of straw used in bricks.

The Great Pyramid was built at a very early time in Egypt's recorded history and, strangely enough for such a huge monument, is not referred to by contemporaneous writers but described by Greeks and Romans who came thousands of years later as tourists. The early history of Egypt, in fact, contains a strange anomaly, for its period of superior culture seemed to evolve at once, about the end of the fourth millennium B.C., from a previous neolithic culture, without any appreciable evidence of the usual transitional stages. It did not evolve, it just occurred—tools, techniques, art, architecture, engineering, medicine, science, and organization of huge cities seems to have suddenly taken place, almost as if it had been imported from some other region, although as far as history tells us, Egypt's civilization is roughly contemporaneous with the other beginnings in the Middle East, which in any case do not resemble it.

But this first burst of civilization, exemplified in the Great Pyramid, did not develop much further and eventually seemed to retrogress, just as the early cultures of South and Central America seem to have been stronger, more vital, and more technically advanced when they started than when they were 'discovered' by the Spaniards. It is almost as if they had received an initial 'infusion' of the techniques of civilization from somewhere else, an impulse which through the centuries became diluted and lost its initial force.

One of the most detailed and thought-provoking studies of the pyramid was recently made by Peter Tomkins—'Secrets of the Great Pyramid'—*Horizon* (winter 1971). He concludes that the pyramid was, among other things, an observatory and also, because of its longitudinal indications, a key to 'a scale map of the northern hemisphere.' In one of his statements about geodesic and scientific capability of the builders he makes a most cogent observation:

Whoever built the Great Pyramid knew, as the legends

accurately report, how to make excellent charts of the stars with which to correctly calculate longitude, draw maps of the globe, and so travel at will across its continents and oceans.

There would seem to be a distinct relation between the background knowledge of whatever people caused the Great Pyramid to be built and the cartographers who drew the original sea maps more ancient than the then extant maps of the world and, at the same time, so much more exact and far encompassing.

If we adopt the supposition that an ancient race once evolved an advanced culture at a distant epoch, as is told in so many legends of so many unrelated peoples, little would have come down to us in any case in the shape of identifiable artifacts or records, considering the lapse of time, destruction by man, decay, climate changes, and modifications of levels of the earth and sea. If knowledge were to survive it would have to be on records so big as to be practically indestructible or be so useful that it would somehow continue to be used and copied, however imperfectly, simply because people needed it to travel safely.

The first requirement is fulfilled by the Great Pyramid and the second by the medieval copies of the ancient maps of the world.

CHAPTER FIVE

THE IMPOSSIBLE BUILDINGS

In attempting to trace the vestiges of a prehistoric civilization down through time, we get the impression that we receive or hear only its echoes, these we perceive in surviving legends, in copies of maps, each recopying losing a certain clarity, interpretations of measures, unexplained bits of scientific information held out of the time progress continuum. But is there nothing else? Are there any buildings or vestiges of buildings that would indicate techniques that would clearly differentiate them from other more easily explainable ancient ruins?

Considering the passage of time as evidenced in the information passed on in the ancient sea maps, especially those dealing with an ice-free Antarctic continent, twelve to fifteen thousand years would have elapsed between the closing days of this hypothetical culture and the present, along with important climatic changes throughout the world. Iron or steel, if such peoples had any, would have disappeared. Wood structures would have vanished. Brick buildings, however huge, would have deteriorated so far as to be indistinguishable from hills or small mountains, as has been the case in Mesopotamia where enormous metropolitan areas, even Babylon itself, had been 'lost' until the fairly recent present, simply because their soil or sand covered ruins were no longer recognizable. In Central and South America this process of recognizing hills or mountains as artificial is still continuing, largely with the help of the airplane.

Identifiable ruins of a prehistoric civilization may be preserved for us under the mile-deep ice of Antarctica, for if Antarctica had once been of sufficient interest for navigators to carefully map its ice-free coastline, offshore islands, rivers, and mountains, it is fairly logical to assume that people lived there and engaged in commerce—always a good reason for making maps. Such prehistoric evidence, however, is presently unavailable to us, unless deep drilling in the Antarctic uncovers vestiges of former habitation, as shallower earth moving by bulldozers in Alaska, Arctic Canada, and Siberia have unearthed from the permafrost frozen saber-tooth tigers, prehistoric horses, mastodons and other non-Arctic animals as well as extensive ancient settlements of almost city size, such as those of Point Barrow, and Port Hope, Alaska. At a site near Port Hope evidences of a considerably advanced prehistoric Arctic culture included tombs still containing skeletons with ivory eyeballs inserted in the eye sockets of their skulls.

Prehistoric building complexes will most probably be identified under the seas and oceans, for cultures and perhaps whole continents have subsided or been engulfed. Such discoveries will probably become increasingly frequent in the future with the development of new underwater research equipment and vehicles.

But there do exist some buildings, or parts of buildings, neither under the ice nor under the sea which, although relatively inaccessible, may represent a link between prehistoric and modern civilization. These massive ruins might well be termed 'the impossible buildings,' because their construction by truly primitive peoples would be impossible with the techniques we suppose them to have had at their command.

Such ruins are found in various places throughout the world. In each case the indigenous inhabitants profess ignorance of who built them, except to ascribe them to a race of supermen, giants, or the gods.

In South America, high on the Andean plateau, on mountain-tops, perched on the edge of thousand-foot-high precipices, and even on desolate desert plateaus so high men and animals experience difficulty in breathing, there are cyclopean ruins which are simply unexplainable without predicating the most modern of stone cutting tools and means of transportation.

The Spanish conquerors found Inca cities, forts, and palaces built on the foundations and surviving walls of previous cultures. These walls are still standing, often with subsequent Inca modifications still in evidence. The mysterious race or races who preceded the Incas were apparently not only able to cut and fit enormous monoliths, but they carried the red porphory blocks somehow from incredible distances across mountains, over rivers and mountain torrents sometimes from quarries more than 1000 miles away, depositing them on cliffs and mountaintops such as Ollantayparubo, Peru, almost as if they had flown them there, as the legends have suggested. Some of these hard andesite and granite rocks weight from 150 to 200 tons. Many are covered with intricate carvings, also the case with the huge stone buildings and stellae, high commemorative free standing pillars, like obelisks, in the Maya lands of Central America.

Hyatt Verrill, considering the stone chipping implements that were apparently used, has commented:

No living man, Indian or otherwise, could ... duplicate the simplest of their stone carvings by means of the stone implements we find. It is not a question of skill, patience, time—it is a human impossibility.

But the carvings were almost a minor feature of the surprising buildings, buildings we can still examine but whose explanation is as far away from us as ever.

Anyone who has visited the Inca ruins in Peru or Bolivia has had pointed out to him the many angled monoliths of palaces, forts, and temples, constructed with stones so closely fitted together that the thinnest gauge cannot be fitted between them. Some stones are more or less rectangular and some have as many as thirty-two angled planes and each fits *exactly* with the next touching stones, from all sides including the *inner* surfaces. The reason for their peculiar 'lock-in' may have been to make them earthquake-proof, as indeed they seem to have been, outlasting many of the later Spanish structures built on them which have tumbled down through the years in the recurring Andean earthquakes.

How were they cut, by what means were the huge stones transported up mountains, and finally, how were they fitted together? They would have had to be fitted in the wall, taken out, cut, placed in again and again to measure for a perfect fit. But the whole stone system interlocks and dovetails, making this laborious process impossible, even if the pre-Incas had possessed the stone cutting tools necessary for the exact degree of accuracy.

As far as is known, no precision stone shaping implements or machines capable of making such multiple fitting of great stones were known to the ancient South Americans and, for this reason, persistent legends and rumours imply that the ancient builders had developed a 'secret ingredient'—a radio-active plant extract which would eat into and dissolve stone, making it fuse itself together or, at least, making the edges malleable. Such an invention, if it existed, would explain the incredible fitting of huge rocks, the intricacy of the handsome carvings, which could have been *molded*, and even the Incan road building, which plunged 3000-mile roads through mountains, canyons, and all sorts of impossible barriers in a direct line.

Colonel P. H. Fawcett, the explorer of South American jungles and student of pre-Columbian civilizations who disappeared in Brazil in 1925 while searching for a lost, but still presumably inhabited, city in the approximate area of the Xingú River in the Amazon tributary system, was of the opinion that the prehistoric builders could soften stones and 'stack' them something like malleable bags of sand or moist cement so that they would flow together and harden, or be pushed together like soft putty.

Fawcett recounted an incident reported from Peru according to which some American mining engineers, while prospecting one of the innumerable *huacas* (burial mounds) near Cerro de Pasco, found a sealed container of the kind also called *huaca* (usually made in the shape of a human head, a human body or an animal) which the Inca and pre-Inca peoples used to store liquids, gold dust, corn kernels, or anything that poured.

Finding some liquid in the *huaca* they tried to force one of the Indian workers with them to drink it. He resisted fearfully and violently, breaking the *huaca* in the process, and ran away. When the engineers returned from a half-hearted pursuit of their victim they noticed that the rock where the *huaca* had broken and spilled had become soft and malleable, before subsequently hardening.

If rock-softening liquids can be made from certain plants (and some jungle plants long known to the Indians have yielded unsuspected treasures or stunning poisons, such as curare) the plants have not been identified, although, according to Fawcett, we have an indication of approximately what they look like. A further report tells of a man who, walking through the forest to get his horse, found that his long spurs had melted around the rowels. When he arrived at the *chacra* or ranch where he had been heading and pointed out the eaten-away spurs, he was asked whether he had walked through a series of low plants with thick red leaves which, in the opinion of the people he spoke to, were the plants used by the Incas for softening rocks.

Even more unusual is Fawcett's report that small birds in the Andes peck out holes for themselves in solid rocks over rushing water courses. Fawcett observed that the birds went about their work first by rubbing the rock with a leaf and then pecking at it.

It is to be remarked that Colonel Fawcett never succeeded in getting a specimen of this leaf nor is it explained why such a powerful softening agent would not soften the jars which held it, the legs of a horse going through it, or as Ivan Sanderson, naturalist and explorer, observes, the beak of the bird holding the leaf.

However they were built, these puzzling monuments still stand on mountaintops and almost inaccessible cliffs. In a sense they confront us with an archaelogical *fait accompli*: they could not have been built—nevertheless, they are there!

The 'impossible' feature of Tiahuanaco, a city of gigantic

ruins on the shore of Lake Titicaca, Bolivia, is that it was built at all. It stands on a desolate plateau at an altitude of 13,000 feet, a height which causes *soroche*, the dizzying mountain sickness, to people unaccustomed to such heights. Its location is too high for corn to grow, for cats to live, for white women to give birth, and certainly too high for a population large enough to have built and carved the enormous stones that comprise the city. In spite of the incredible altitude a large population must have once lived in the vicinity, as evinced by the terraced hillsides, a deserted port, and extensive ruins nearby.

When the Spaniards arrived at Tiahuanaco the Quechua and Aymará Indians they found were unable to tell them much about the vast deserted city, except that it was built by the gods. Upon close examination the Spaniards found that the enormous stone walls of the temples, set upon foundations blocks weighing as much as 100 tons each, were held in place by silver tenons. The Spanish discoverers enthusiastically removed these tenons in a large-scale construction (or destruction) operation of their own. Unfortunately many of the walls collapsed in subsequent earthquakes and a large section of the city, including carved stones and statues, was literally carted away over centuries to make other buildings, including much of the city of La Paz, and also to furnish a roadbed for a railroad. Most of the material remaining was simply too massive to be transported.

Nevertheless, enough remains to furnish an archaeological puzzle. Not only is it incredible that such elaborate carvings could have been made on hard stone with stone tools, but that the building stones are cut geometrically true, as if they had been shaped by steel tools. A stone gate still standing, called by present-day Indians the Door of the Sun (although the central figure is thought to be the Rain God) is cut from a single giant stone and deeply carved with enigmatic figures, some of which are unfinished, as if something interrupted the work of the carvers.

The age of Tiahuanaco is a subject of controversy, varying from 1500 to 15,000 or more years. Bones of extinct animals

82

found nearby do not necessarily indicate the age of the city. However, when drawings of extinct animals, such as the toxodon, appear on fragments of pottery, a definite basis for lengthening the time span of such a site is indicated. It has often been suggested that Tiahuanaco, a port which is now away from the water and Lake Titicaca, a deep lake with oceanic fauna, were once at sea level and were thrust more than two miles upward during a convulsion of the earth which also

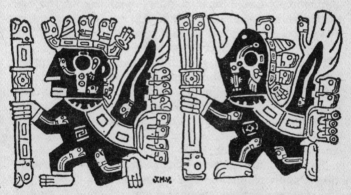

Figures engraved on the Gate of the Sun shown on page 52. Some investigators of these figures have suggested that ancient counterparts of modern inventions may be seen in these (and other) survivals of antiquity, pointing out that the eye motif of the figure on the left looks like a deep sea deep diver or an astronaut, while the eye motif of the bird-like figure on the right resembles a jet-propelled vehicle.

formed the 'new' chain of the Andes, a theory which would tend to explain the abandonment of Tiahuanaco and the existence of a 'salt' line on the surrounding mountains.

The origin of Tiahuanaco is so mysterious, its setting so desolate, its construction so unexplainable that some researchers who have remained long enough to accustom themselves to the altitude have deepened the mystery of Tiahuanaco through their conclusions.

Some of these refer to the Gate of the Sun. The central anthropomorphic figure above the gate has rays surrounding its head and holds in each hand what may be symbolic bolts of lightning. It is flanked by twenty-four minor figures facing it on each side, some man-like and some bird-like. These may have a calendar or astronomical function as is so often the case with Amerindian carvings. A very close look, however, at the headdresses and face carvings of some of the subordinate figures provides some startling resemblances. The upturned eye of one of the bird-like creatures seems to be part of a jet-propelled aircraft or underwater vehicle, while the eye of one of the man-like creatures seems to form part of a pictorial representation of a 'hard-hat' diver. These suggested similarities possess an added significance partly because of the legends of 'gods from the sky' descending at Tiahuanaco and also because of the rumors of the existence of great ruins under the surface of Lake Titicaca which, however, Captain Cousteau failed to note during his submarine exploration of part of the lake bottom.

As a result of the lack of written records, or at least records that we can read, certain enormous mountains of the Americas may not be definitely recognized even today—not because they are lost, but because they are so tremendous. Such is the case with the Panecillo ('bread roll'), a mountain outside Quito, Ecuador, which owes its name to the fact that it is shaped somewhat like an upended bread roll. Ever since Quito, as the northern capital of the Inca Empire, was seized by the Spanish and after burning, rebuilt, digging has been going on intermittently on the Panecillo because of the usual rumors of Inca gold, silver, or jewels hidden there. Within the last decade or so, however, it has become increasingly apparent, through study of its stratigraphy, or rather its lack of strata, that the Panecillo is not a mountain at all but some sort of enormous artificial mound built so long before the Incas that there is not even a legend concerning it. Excavations on the top have partially revealed a curious beehive stone construction somewhat resembling a Bessemer converter or an inverted modern cesspool, with no indication of what it really is or why it was built.

Throughout the length of the Americas many other mountains and hills, overgrown and unrecognized for centuries have turned out to be man-made pyramids or mounds. We know the hill on which the Church of Cholula, Mexico, is built was an Aztec pyramid-temple platform, over 200 feet high and covering considerably more space than the Great Pyramid of Egypt.

The highest building in the Americas, before the construction of New York's first skyscrapers, was a forgotten Mayan temple in Tikal, Guatemala, now simply designated as Tikal IV. Tikal IV, covered by trees, was 'lost' for centuries in the jungle, although, shaped more like a steep tower than a pyramid, it soared to a height of 212 feet. Similarly, huge pyramid-like palaces, temples, and forts on the Peruvian coast, made of clay bricks, have been thought because of their size to be natural features of the terrain, until surrounding constructions, visible in outline from the air, although not from the ground, have shown them to be man-made centers, belonging to the pre-Inca Chimú and other cultures. In Mexico, during the revolutionary period, Pancho Villa's soldiers once established an artillery post on a flat-topped hill from which to bombard the Federal Army. Their constant fire shook off some of the covering earth of the top of an Aztec pyramid on which they were standing.

Some other natural features of the American continent may lead us to surprising discoveries. Hills and cliffs in some parts of the Amazon suspiciously resemble man-made constructions. In the Marcahuasi plateau of Peru, large sections of mountain rock have been carved and modified into the form of human faces, lions, camels, and what appear to be alligators, hippopotamuses and also something closely resembling a prehistoric stegasaurus. These carvings are recognizable only at certain times, such as the summer equinox, when the sun, striking them exactly right, brings out their complete features. A seismic cracking of a mountain wall in Paraguay in 1947 revealed an inner 'worked' wall about 120 feet high and continuing for almost a mile but, like other 'illogical' South

American remains, its huge size and inaccessibility makes detailed examination difficult and makes it easier to classify it as a 'natural' wonder.

Obviously it is easy to imagine natural formations into buildings or to exaggerate what one has seen. This may be the case with the huge limestone pillars in Australia, 30 miles north of the Roper River, rumored in legend to have been the work of members of a white race who landed in Australia thousands of years ago, and the recurrent reports during World War II by U.S. airmen that in China, within about 40 miles of Sian-fu in Shensi Province there were enormous pyramids made of earth approximately twice as tall as those of Egypt, with a base side of 1500 feet. Photographs of these 'pyramids' are reported to be filed in Air Force archives but have not been made public. (A natural human tendency to 'see' terrain features as artifacts has even occurred on the moon where Russian reports reprinted in the Soviet magazine *Technology of Youth* suggest the presence of planned structures on the moon, allegedly photographed on February 4, 1966, by the Russian Lunar Probe IX over the Ocean of Storms, showing an arrangement of 'stone markers,' and a Russian intepretation of U.S. photographs 29 miles over the Sea of Tranquility showing a collection of spires or 'pointed pyramids,' one of which was estimated by the Russian scientist, Dr. Ivanov, from shadows cast, as being 15 stories high.)

Actual monuments such as the obelisks, temples, and pyramids of Egypt are equally mysterious in regard to the indications of stored knowledge they may contain but their features of actual construction and transportation of material has been drawn for succeeding generations by the ancient Egyptians themselves. Enormous blocks were quarried by use of expanding wedges, lifted by pulleys or pulled and pushed on rollers or great sleds which, in turn, ran on smooth greased runways. Obelisks apparently were hauled up ramps and tipped into sand-filled holes which, as the sand was taken out, righted the obelisks and set them in place.

It is now generally considered that the stones of the Great Pyramid were pulled into place over a huge ramp whose height varied according to the level—finally an earth ramp the height of the pyramid itself—almost 50 stories at its original level. If this is true, then the figure quoted by Herodotus that the pyramids were built by 100,000 men working twenty years should perhaps be modified considerably upward, considering the time for quarrying and transporting the stone blocks, personnel to supply the multitude of workers with food and water, the constructing and constant repairing and changing the 'skyscraper' earth ramp, the delicate and exact measurements to be taken and finally, putting the blocks in place and facing them with limestone. Even though the pyramids are not 'impossible' (an Arab foreman of a thirty-man team once observed to the archaeologist Reisner while putting a block weighing several tons back on the third pyramid, using rollers, ropes, and levers—'If we are so ordered we can build a pyramid') there is still a certain measure of incredibility in the precise setting of such masses of stone as well as the knowledge and reasoning behind it.

The mystery of how the great lava-stone statues at Easter Island were put into place has been partially solved by Thor Heyerdahl, during his investigations there. On Easter Island, isolated in the Pacific 2350 miles off the coast of Chile, are almost six hundred enormous stone statues, called *moai*, showing the torsos and heads of enigmatic figures, some of which measure about four stories in height and weigh up to 50 tons each. They were originally set on stone platforms and on their flat heads were balanced huge red-colored stone topknots which were cut and transported from a distant quarry. Most of these statues had been tipped over, losing their topknots, and others had their phalluses broken off. Still others lay in the original quarry where they were evidently still being produced when some disaster overtook their sculptors.

The native population of Easter Island, numbering only several thousand when it was first discovered in 1722 (and subsequently reduced by Peruvian slavers in the nineteeth century to as few as one hundred), was considered to be too small for mass production of colossi and it has been suggested that Easter Island was once a part of a larger land mass which could have, as in the case of Egypt, furnished the necessary number of labourers. Indeed, it semed impossible for the inhabitants to have transported the stones into position, to have set them upright and to have subsequently set the red topknots on their heads, a fairly difficult operation even with modern machinery.

However, Thor Heyerdahl, once he had gained their confidence, found that there still existed vestiges of a tradition among the Easter Islanders concerning the lifting of the stone statues and he was able to photograph the raising of one, done through many workers using long poles as levers, ropes, and piles of smaller rocks acting as fulcrum and also as support. The psychological preparation of the workers was carried out through songs and ceremonies over a night-long period (including a ritual dance by a virgin) enabling them to work in unison and in perfect harmony. What still remains to be ascertained, however, is why their ancestors built so many figures and also why building was suddenly suspended. Local legends tell of wars between tribes and castes, decimation and massacre finally ending in cannibalism, a sort of *descensus averni* of a formerly developed culture.

A similar system of levers, ropes, and holding stones must have been used to raise the stone pillars of Stonehenge, on the Salisbury Plain in England, as well as the thousands of stone menhirs (standing stones) and dolmens (great stone slabs set on other stones) in Brittany in France.

The prehistoric stone constructions seem to be concentrated along the Atlantic and Mediterranean coasts and islands although they extend through Europe as far as the Ural Mountains of Russia. Some are enormous—one tomb in France is roofed by stones weighing more than 80 tons apiece. A standing stone erected at Locmariquer, Brittany, measured 65 feet high when it stood upright, and weighed 342 tons.

The construction of the enormous roofed stone circles of Stonehenge with architectural features such as tenons and mortice holes cut in the stone shows some relationship to the megalithic stonework of Tiahuanaco and other pre-Inca ruins of South America, not only in some of its construction details but perhaps also in the reasons for its being built—the construction of a gigantic seasonal or astronomical clock with perhaps other features that we have not yet discovered.

There are some indications, from finds of 'imported' jewelry and weapons *in situ*, that representatives of a more advanced race may have contributed the know-how for the erection of Stonehenge and other sites and perhaps to have aided in the measurements according to which the sun would rise directly over the 'heel stone,' marking the main axis of Stonehenge, at the beginning of summer, June 21. Since the position of the earth and the sun has slightly shifted since the time Stonehenge was built, it has been calculated that the day that the sun passed *exactly* over the heel stone was in the area of 200 B.C. A similar slight discrepancy in positioning the sun's rays for the equinox has been noted in the pre-Incan sanctuary at Machu Picchu in the Andes, still called *intihuatana*—'the hitching post of the sun.'

Other transoceanic resemblances, not necessarily in style, but in apparent purpose occur—a huge stone zodiacal calendar at Glastonbury, a circle of 30 miles in circumference near Stonehenge, was apparently meant to be seen from above. Its age is not known but what is thought to be contemporaneous settlements in the immediate vicinity give a carbon dating of 20,000 years. Another huge prehistory pictograph of uncertain age or purpose exists on a hillside in Dorset, reminding one of the 'Candelabra of the Andes' of Peru.

The great temple of Avebury, in Wiltshire, is said to have been much larger than Stonehenge, having once had 650 giant stones forming a great circle around an artificial hill, but through the years its stones have been broken up for building with only twenty left standing.

On the large plain of Carnac, Brittany, there are hundreds of standing stones set in perfectly straight lines. These may have functioned as a calendar, a system of counting, a commemoration of chiefs, or some other purpose that we cannot imagine, perhaps connected with astrology. But its scope, as well as that of Stonehenge, while not impossible, suggests that a well organized work system existed in Western Europe in prehistoric times.

In Baalbek, Lebanon, contained within the foundation platform on which is built a Temple of Jupiter belonging to the classical period of archaeology, there are several cyclopean stones whose quarrying and transportation are difficult and almost impossible to explain. The temple platform was constructed by builders who left no record and the Temple of Jupiter was built on it. Along the side of the platform are three enormous 1000 ton stones, larger and heavier than any others ever found in classical buildings, but even they are surpassed by another, quarried but never transported, which weighs no less than 2000 tons.

The illogical hugeness of these stones remind one of the stones of the pre-Inca forts at Sacsahuaman, Cuzco, and other sites. The pre-Incas seemed to use whatever was at hand, without special consideration of the size. In like manner, unless the original builders of the terrace of Baalbek had some way of transporting and placing blocks that we do not know of, would it not have been easier to *cut* such cyclopean stones and then place them? The Egyptian obelisks, heavy as they were, were meant to be one commemorative piece, but these blocks, fitted in with others of more normal size, were simply the terrace foundation for the temple.

Long before the Parthenon was built on the Acropolis overlooking Athens, cyclopean structures existed there from an earlier age. The word 'cyclopean' comes from Cyclops, the giant blinded by Ulysses and his men during one of their many misadventures on their way back from the Trojan War. The Greeks, noting certain huge megalithic structures in their own lands and in many other islands and coasts of the Mediterranean, considered that they could not have been built by men, but by giants.

We find these megalithic (giant stone) structures throughout the Mediterranean, in Greece, Crete, Asia Minor, Lybia, Sardinia, Pantelleria, Malta, southern Spain, the Balearic Islands, the earliest ruins of Egypt, and occasionally reported on the sea bottom of the Aegean, off Melos and Thera.

By an interesting coincidence, most of these cyclopean

90

ruins are near the sea. The cult of the great stones extends to England, the coasts of France and Portugal, and is especially remarkable in Ireland, where the origin of the great stone forts of Aran is attributed either to giants or to misty people of the sea, who came to Ireland eons ago. Far from Ireland, in Rhodesia, East Africa, there stands the unexplained building complex of Zimbabwe, variously thought to be a palace, temple, fortress, or the gold mines of King Solomon. It is made of cut stone in a land where cut stone, probably since it was not needed, was never used. But a comparison of the walls of Zimbabwe with those of the mysterious Atlantic forts of Ireland suggests that they, as well as other megalithic structures in other parts of the world, principally on islands and seacoasts, were built (or planned) by the same people.

Cyclopean monuments found in the Pacific and Atlantic Oceans, and, in South America, they include the most amazing buildings ever built. Prehistoric archaeological vestiges are not lacking in the Central United States, where thousands of pyramid mounds, some in the shape of animals and reptiles and at least one shaped like an elephant have provided an interesting field of research for centuries. Unfortunately many have been obliterated by early settlers or subsequently by bulldozers. Their origin is still being argued, as to whether they were built by a 'lost' culture or simply made by the ancestors of the Indians, who, victims of a curious regression, 'forgot' about them. In any event, these American mounds or pyramids fit in a general pattern of gigantic mounds which spread all over the world—sometimes called the 'pyramid belt'—from Egypt and Mesopotamia west to Europe and the Americas and east to India, Central Asia, China, Indonesia, and other South Pacific islands.

It is a matter of conjecture whether these enormous mounds were inspired by a common source such as Sumeria, Egypt, or even an earlier culture that has disappeared, or were simply the result of a shared natural urge to build a lasting tomb, or to set up a temple 'in the high places' connected with sun worship or astronomy.

Recent finds, or even re-evaluations of past finds in the

United States, may indicate the presence of megalithic culture other than Indian mounds or the adobe or cliff-dweller culture of the Southwest. These 'second thoughts' are being examined in such unexpected places as New England, where megalithic-looking structures in New Hampshire and various other sites in the Atlantic states may have been unrecognized for centuries since they had been used as foundations or incorporated into new buildings by the early settlers who, being interested in survival or comfort rather than archaeology, did not question the origin of these structures, but simply made use of them.

The United States, long regarded archaeologically as a sort of 'parvenu' among nations, may yet reserve some surprises for the studies of prehistory. Since no outstanding indigenous culture was found in what is now the eastern United States, however, it has been generally accepted that there never was one or traces would have been found, especially along the coast, as has been the case in so many other regions.

Recently, off the coast of the United States, preserved in the world's great conservatory of the past, the ocean, what appear to be megalithic structures, some of cyclopean rocks, have been sighted, visited by divers, and photographed. As this book goes to press these unexpected finds are even now in the process of further investigation and may eventually influence the whole concept of the possibility of sunken lands, the age of civilized man in America, and early communication routes between America and other parts of the world.

CHAPTER SIX

SUNKEN CITIES OFF THE AMERICAN COAST

During the period between the two World Wars the airplane began to make substantial contributions to archaeology, not only through tracing outlines of former cities, walls, and roads from the air because of terrain delineation not noticeable from the ground, but sometimes revealing under the clear waters of the Mediterranean and Aegean Seas fairly complete towns, cities, and harbors either submerged by rising water or having fallen into the sea. To obtain photographs of these sunken ruins from the air, the water must be calm, clear, and with little surface movement; what would be visible from the air one day could be unidentifiable the next. In the Mediterranean and the Aegean chance spotting from the air has produced detailed pictures of Roman villas beneath the sea, the ancient resort city of Baiae, the great Phoenician ports of Tyre and Sidon, and even parts of the original Carthage, whose vestiges on land were so thoroughly obliterated by the Romans. While these sunken cities and ruins were conveniently at hand for thousands of years and no doubt were sporadically visited by free divers looking for sponges, it was not until the advent of the airplane that it was possible to locate, photograph, and plot so many of them and in such detail.

In the Americas such ruins were not located because it never occurred to anyone to look for them. During World War II, however, man-made buildings or other type constructions were sometimes reported by pilots on submarine duty in the Caribbean. The pilots, on look out for submerged objects such as submarines, would occasionally see straight lines and sometimes rectangles under the water, often connected with the land, especially in the vicinity of Mexico, Yucatán, and British

Honduras.

Branching diagonally off the coast between Isla Mujeres and Cozumel, and in the bay between Cozumel and Chetumal and on the coast of Quintana Roo, Mexico, are stone causeways still visible under the water, at a depth of 30 to 100 feet, a continuation of causeways on land which are now completely overgrown by the jungle. These causeways are occasionally visible all the way down to Belize, in British Honduras.

An extensive limestone formation forms a relatively shallow bottom off the coast of Yucatán and notably in the Bahama complex as well. Underwater caves and sinkholes in this area show the formation of stalactites and stalagmites, indicating that the whole area was above sea level at some period in the past. Therefore, it may be reasonable to assume that these causeways, if such they were, led from one Maya city or temple complex to another when they were both on land, although now the land causeway has vanished while its sea extension still leads to other cities now submerged.

A more unusual continuing discovery also initiated from the air has been progressing since 1968 in the Bahamas group, not far from the coast of Florida. These underwater discoveries have been accompanied by a series of extraordinary coincidences, claims, and denials, and may eventually develop into a full-grown archaeological controversy. They concern buildings, temples, walls, roads, ports, and whole cities under the waters of the continental shelf of America.

Underwater ruins and wrecks abound on the Caribbean and Atlantic coasts but hitherto they have concerned Spanish colonizers and their fortresses, Spanish ships sunk by storms or while fleeing from pirates, and finally, vestiges of the pirates themselves. As for one city that sank beneath the sea, we know its name—Port Royal (Jamaica), and the date on which it sank —June 7, 1692, and even the time of its demise, from the gold watch of one of its victims, which understandably stopped during the sudden earthquake which sunk the pirate city with all its inhabitants under six fathoms of water and several feet of mud.

The discoveries in the Bahama waters, however, do not date

94

from colonial times but from an epoch prior to Columbus, perhaps thousands of years ago. There are many possible reasons why they were not sighted until 1968: they may have been covered by sand which uncovered them after a storm; minor earthquakes may have made them more prominent; since there were no rumors of special treasure, no one had searched for them in that part of the ocean; or, perhaps the most logical explanation of all, that no one was looking for them.

The initial circumstances of the Bahama finds which, although increasingly numerous, have not yet been archaeologically verified, came about because two pilots were actually searching, during their routine flights over the Bahama Banks, for the reappearance of a part of Atlantis, the lost continent described by Plato as having sunk into the Atlantic 9000 years before the time of Plato, that is, about 11,500 years before our era. This reappearance of Atlantis (for 1968) had been prophesied by Edgar Cayce in 1923.

During his lifetime, which ended in 1945, Edgar Cayce developed a devoted following through his activities in psychic readings, which solved health problems for people in various parts of the world, many of whom he had never met. His activities led to the establishment of the Edgar Cayce Foundation and the Association for Research and Enlightenment at Virginia Beach, Virginia, which long after his death still attracts members impressed by his healing ability and the content of his prophecies. Some of these prophecies, concerning assassinations of Presidents and expected-to-be Presidents, race riots, earthquakes, and even mud slides in California, proved disturbingly similar to headlines that were still to come, twenty or more years in the future. In the course of his psychic readings we find an increasing number of references to Atlantis and to the reappearance of part of it in 1968.

A most unusual feature of the Cayce readings about Atlantis was that, when he was not in a trance-like state, he was surprised at his repeated references to Atlantis, and was once quoted as saying: 'I wonder where that came from and if there is anything in it?'—a doubt, one might say, widely shared by numerous archaeologists. Nevertheless he continued to refer to Atlantis in his readings, saying in 1933 that '...A portion of the temple [of Atlantis] may yet be discovered under the slime of ages of sea water—near what is known as Bimini, off the coast of Florida.' Later, in 1940, he made an exact prediction of the reappearance of part of the western section of Atlantis exactly twenty-eight years in the future: 'And Poseidia will be among the first portions of Atlantis to rise again. Expect it in sixty-eight and sixty-nine ('68 and '69). Not so far away!'

The unusual aspect, therefore, of the first sightings reported off Andros Island is that the pilots who first saw them, Robert Brush and Trigg Adams, were members of the Association for Research and Enlightenment and, during their regular flying duties, were keeping one eye open for confirmation of Cayce's prophecy. Naturally, what seems like revelation to the people who believe in Cayce's prophecies seems like pure coincidence to those who view all unfamiliar phenomena with a coldly scientific eye.

The initial underwater find off the Island of Andros, near Pine Key, in 1968 was rectangular construction outlined by beach grass and sponges fairly near the surface divided into several sections by stone partitions. The vestigial walls continue on down beneath the sand and the flooring, if any, has not yet been found.

Believers in Atlantis, mindful of Cayce's references to the location of Atlantis, such as '...the Bahamas are a portion ... that may be seen in the present ...' interpreted this 1968 sighting as fulfillment of his prophecy, and considered the building to be an Atlantean temple, literally rising from the sea.

Others, while recognizing that the mysterious rectangle is some sort of man-made construction and cognizant of the fact that the local Carib Indians at the time of the discovery of America did not build in stone, have labeled it a Spanish blockhouse (although not explaining why it is underwater), a fish trap (although it would seem an unduly complicated one to be made of stone and exactly measured), or even a storage pen for conch shells, sponges, or turtles. The suggestion of use as a turtle pen has caused further confusion in view of the incredible coincidence arising from the fact that the floor plan of the building is similar to that of the 'Temple of the Turtles' in Uxmal, Yucatán.

As more aerial photographs were taken of the area, more underwater 'buildings' were found nearby, suggesting the vestiges of a settlement or town or, as their numbers grow, a small city. As discovery and investigation continue, along with efforts to protect these finds from treasure hunters who would like to dynamite them to see what lies beneath, only one thing seems fairly certain and that is that the builders did not construct these buildings underwater and their present submarine location indicates a subsidence of what once was dry land.

Other evidences of what may have been harbor works prior to the discovery of America existed in Miami on the south shore of the Miami River in the shape of a large circular hole near the 'prehistoric' beach line, expanding down in a perfect circle cut into the beach rock for about 60 feet, the sides showing indications of tool marks. It may be noted that circular inner harbors were a mark of Carthaginian harbor construction. Whatever it was, it is now filled in and what may have been a prehistoric harbor work is concealed under an apartment house across from the Dupont Plaza. Another ancient construction, a canal also showing tool marks on the reef rock walls is still traceable underwater at Key Largo, Florida. Even more unusual was the discovery, also in 1968, of what appears to be a cyclopean stone construction about 35 feet under the water and about 1000 yards from the shore of North Bimini, through the initial efforts of Dr. Manson Valentine, anthropologist and archaeologist, Dimitri Rebikoff, inventor and underwater archaeologist, and Jacques Mayol, holder of the world's depth record for free diving. This series of enormous stones, first referred to as a road, because the huge stone blocks seen from above seemed to be paving stones, is now considered in the opinion of its finders to be a wall, either thrown over on its side by some convulsion of nature or perhaps the foundation of a vanished building or even the top of a massive wall which is still buried in the sand. There are indications that the stonework extends much farther than the exposed portion which has been photographed and studied, perhaps even forming a girdling wall around part or the whole island of North and South Bimini.

This time contrary opinion did not label the wall a turtle pen but generally suggested that the stones were natural features, the result of faulting of the sea bed. However, inspection of the regular shape of the wall and the apparent joining together of the stones as well as their striking resemblance to the pre-Inca masonry of Peru makes a convincing case for their man-made origin to anyone who has seen them.

As underwater investigations proceed in the Bimini area, new finds are being constantly reported, sometimes to be lost again, however, when they become recovered by the shifting bottom sands before they can be investigated. Moreover, the discoverers of what may be ruins or artifacts are understandably reticent to pinpoint their discoveries in order to retain control of the investigation of their discoveries, a tendency not necessarily limited to underwater archaeology alone.

Among some of the more sensational discoveries reported is the account of a charter boat captain that he had discovered a 'step pyramid' at a depth of 12 fathoms. Other walls have been sighted on the bottom; fossilized mangrove roots on a 300-foot-long wall gave carbon dated readings of 6000 to 12,000 years. Dimitri Rebikoff is reported to have found a wall built around what is now a fresh water spring, a suggestion to the imagination that it was a garden pool before the land sank.

Sightings are continuing from the air; especially since pilots are looking for vestiges of underwater constructions. At least a dozen have been sighted in the Andros area, and numerous others far out at sea, although still on the Bahama Banks. As reported by Robert Marks, diver, underwater explorer, and archaeologist, a PAA pilot who, perhaps through an understandable desire to avoid implications of divided attention, 'wants to remain anonymous,' told Marks that he had discovered still another wall in fairly deep water (12 fathoms) off Bimini which had 'a large archway going through the middle of it.' If the pilot saw the wall from the air—perfectly possible with the presence of certain conditions tending to produce an unruffled surface of the sea, it would still be difficult, of course, to discern an archway if the observer were not actually under the water. In addition, a pre-Columbian archway would call for a reappraisal of American archaeological theory, as no true arch was apparently known to the Amerinds.

Finds such as these have caused considerable re-examination of the waters of the Great Bahama Banks and farther out at sea in much deeper waters a larger building, occasionally referred to as an underwater pyramid, has been located. It is reported to measure 180 by 140 feet. If it is a pyramid it is a truncated one or a temple platform of which only the top may be showing.

In the understandable enthusiasm of diving for remains of ancient civilizations under the Atlantic Ocean care must be taken not to convert wishes or assumptions into conclusions. Some 'ancient' stone columns from the sea bottom near Bimini turned out upon examination to be cylindrical cement ballast. More recently, however, divers have sighted, in somewhat deeper water, fluted stone columns as well as stone supports, still standing, raised on pillars, comparable in construction to docks and ports of the ancient Mediterranean, where stone construction permitted free wave action under the docks.

Nevertheless, the more one examines the waters of the Bahamas and the Caribbean the more man-made constructions of what might be, according to their shape, buildings, walls, causeways, streets, plazas, and harbor works seem to appear and not always near shore but sometimes hundreds of miles at sea. There is even a recent report of a marble citadel or acropolis, covering four or five undersea acres, with roads leading from it to unknown destinations. This last discovery poses a question for American skindivers since it lies in waters not too remote from visits by Cuban patrol boats.

Underwater buildings or walls, antedating any presently held historic records, have been reported at other points off the coast of the United States, as well as in some of its inland lakes. One of especial interest is located off Brenton's Point, Newport, Rhode Island, where, in 1935, a Navy diver ('hard hat'—i.e. non-scuba), descending to clear a wire drag for recovering torpedoes, found a mound with walls and masonry on its summit at a depth of about 40 feet. Speculation inferred that if it were a relatively modern lighthouse base there would be some record of it since only in fairly recent periods has it been possible to build lighthouses so far at sea, by the preliminary sinking of steel caissons down to the ocean bed, in this case about a mile offshore. Records of the Coast Guard do not reveal any lighthouse construction in the Brenton Reef area. However, if the construction were a thousand, or several thousand years old, the present bottom may have been above sea level.

Several divers have attempted underwater research on this construction since it was first noted, the most sensational firsthand account being furnished in 1958 by a scuba diver, Jackson Jenks, who reported that the building was a tower, 'conical in shape, 50–60 feet high, 40–50 feet in diameter, with the top about 40 feet below the surface ... built of quarried uncemented stones, each as big as an office desk, with a parapet encircling the top ... (and) a door seemed to be set in the saucer shaped top ...' The exact location of the tower is not yet marked by surface buoy, nor have exact coordinates for public knowledge been furnished by divers, a somewhat general practice in undersea exploration throughout the world, where finders of sites or treasures tend to experience a protective interest in their discoveries.

An amazing report which may concern the above or other underwater remains came from fishermen in the mid 1960s when an early-morning fishing party, during a phenomenally low tide passed, *north* of Newport, on their way to the fishing grounds, a barnacle encrusted masonry arch coming out of the sea. They neglected to mark it, and search for this arch as well as the tower is still being pursued by the New England Archaeological Research Association (NEARA). It has been suggested that these reported underwater stone constructions were built by the Northmen who are generally supposed to have built the round stone tower of uncertain origin in Newport, although another school of thought attribute it to (of all people!) Benedict Arnold's grandfather. But, while there is a record that he once owned it as a mill, there is no record of who built an eleventh century European round tower in the colonies, and there it still stands, an enigmatic survival of what may be the first European building in the Western Hemisphere. Notwithstanding this 'Viking' tower on land, however, it is unlikely that the remains under the sea were constructed at such a recent period, geologically speaking.

Further underwater constructions, awaiting more thorough investigation, located in some inland lakes in New England, as, for example, Meddybemps Lake in Maine, may be the remains of Indian ceremonial centres or prehistoric constructions, either one built at a time when the water level of the lakes as well as the water level of the sea was considerably lower. This is further evidenced by the carving of an ancient galley found on a large boulder in Lake Assawompset, Massachusetts, in 1957, when the lake partially dried up during a severe drought.

A most unusual discovery in the ocean off the coast of Peru in 1966 caused a flurry of archaeological expectation but the report was filed away and never publicly explained or, as far as one can ascertain, never followed up. It concerned an oceanographic research expedition from Duke University under the direction of Dr. Robert Menzies which was specifically searching for a type of sea mollusk in the Milne-Edward Trench off the coast of Peru. In the course of their regular research the expedition's cameras brought up what has been described as photographs of carved columns, strewn over a plain at a depth of about 1000 fathoms. Sonar scanning further revealed stationary masses of some sort of the same vicinity which may have been remnants of other buildings although, in the alleged words of Dr. Menzies '... the idea of a sunken city in the Pacific seems incredible ...' Preliminary inspection of the photographs revealed that the columns were not only carved but gave evidence of what appeared to be written characters incised upon them.

The fact that the columns were photographed at such a depth does not necessarily mean that they were constructed there when and if the land was above water; they may possibly have been columns of Spanish colonial vintage that had sunk with an old Spanish galleon, although the nearby presence of what may be buildings fits in conveniently with the theory of catastrophic land changes in South America. These would be the upheavals that thrust parts of the ancient lowlands thousands of feet upward; which emptied lakes and inland seas, still leaving their tidal marks on the mountains; which turned some mountains inside out, exposing their inner caves and throwing extruded cave sections over mountain plateaus; and which dropped other cities into deep trenches off the new coastline.

The photographs of the carved columns are still on file and no further explanation has been forthcoming nor has, as far as anyone knows, a further expedition attempted to retrieve any of them, perhaps understandable considering the expense of such an operation which would be somewhat comparable to the retrieval of the atom bomb recently sunk off Palomares, Spain, by the midget submarine *Alvin*.

Seen from underwater, natural shapes often seem to be buildings or wrecks while true wrecks or remains of buildings are often unrecognized except by a practiced eye. In addition, things happen so quickly underwater and conditions are so ephemeral because of shifting currents as well as one's own speed of locomotion that unusual objects are sometimes glimpsed once, usually in the course of another mission, and then cannot be found again. An example of this is the mysterious stairway noticed in 1964 by French naval officers during a deep dive of the bathyscope *Archimède*. Looking out the porthole Captain Houot and Lieutenant de Froberville saw, as they were lowered down the precipitous edge of the underwater shelf, what appeared to be clearly identifiable as a flight of cut stone steps leading down toward the lower depths. Such formations seen quickly underwater may of course be scientifically explained by flaking or chipping of the underwater cliff, such as can be seen in the Giant's Causeway—a series of flat-topped jutting rocks above and below the water off the coast of Ireland built by giants of misty Gaelic legend—although the technical preparation of the officers should preclude the possibility of such flights of fancy.

A casual examination of a depth map of the ocean around the Bahamas delineates a land mass which is generally considered to have been above sea level during the last Ice Age, when so much of the earth's water was frozen into the alternately advancing and retreating glaciers of the North. This enormous island, basically limestone, was indented by sections of the true ocean, including the underwater canyon called Tongue of the Ocean, which penetrates deep into the Bahama Banks directly east of Andros, where the water falls vertiginously from a relatively shallow depth of 15 or 20 feet to over 4000 feet. In this cliff are the famous 'blue holes,' cavelike underwater openings in the limestone cliff which sometimes lead into underwater passages thought by some of the divers who have tentatively explored them to go on for miles. That these caves were once above water level is evident by the presence of stalagmites and stalactites within them.

If the whole Bahama Banks area, except for the indentations of the true ocean, was above sea level about 12,000 years ago, it is possible to expect that vestiges of human occupation or carving will eventually be found in some of these underwater caves, as has been done in similar formations on the Florida coast. The presence of underwater ruins in this part of the Atlantic and the Caribbean would have the same explanation; they were constructed on dry land which was subsequently engulfed when the ice melted at an accelerated rate. This evident explanation might be further applied to allegedly 'lost' lands in other parts of the ocean, as we approach the borderline where legend becomes history.

CHAPTER SEVEN

LOST CONTINENTS AND THE BOTTOM OF THE SEA

Certain surviving writings of the ancient world that have come down to us demonstrate a generally prevalent belief that, while new lands sometimes rose from the sea bottom, old lands often sank into the sea, obliterating former civilizations in the process.

Egyptian priests, who had long known of the presence of fossil marine shells in the Nile Valley and surrounding hills, informed the travelling historian Herodotus (484 B.C.) about this when he visited Egypt. He coupled this fact with his own evaluation of the salt constitution of Egyptian rocks and deduced that the part of Egypt near the Mediterranean had once been covered by the sea.

Xanthus (500 B.C.), a historian of the Greek city of Sardis, in Asia Minor, noted the presence of fossil shells in the mountains of Armenia and Asia Minor and concluded that the bed of the ocean and the land were constantly changing positions. Another Greek observer from Asia Minor, Xenophones, in discussing recurrent sinkings and catastrophes makes mention of prehistoric impressions of laurel leaves in rocks found by the sea, as indications of a submerged forest.

In his famous *Metamorphosis*, Ovid (43 B.C.) mentions, in what may be a reference to the former separation of Sicily from the Italian mainland: 'I saw what was formerly solid land was a strait and lands formed from the level sea ...' Apuleius, a Latin writer of the second century A.D., in *De Mundo* comments: 'Lands which before were continents have been changed into islands and others, which had been islands, have been changed into continents by the withdrawal of the sea ...' The Greeks and Romans knew, moreover, that certain historic cities had, through earthquakes, literally fallen into the sea. One such city, Heliké in the Gulf of Corinth, was still visible from the surface in classical times, with its underwater streets and villas fairly intact, and was frequently visited by tourists of ancient times, who looked at it from boats, and free divers dove down to its submerged streets for sponges and occasionally retrieved 'antiques.'

Among the different sunken lands referred to in antiquity as centers of great civilization there have survived numerous references to lands or mysterious islands in the Atlantic Ocean, past the Pillars of Hercules, at the entrance to (or exit from) the Mediterranean, sometimes called Atlantis or similar sounding names such as Antilla or referred to as the Fortunate Islands, Islands of the Blest, the Hesperides, or other names. Such allusions are often concerned with legendary exploits of gods or heroes but one gets a general impression of a powerful empire located out in the Atlantic and land or continents on the other side. Classical allusions are numerous. Homer (born in the eighth century B.C.) wrote in the *Odyssey* about Scheria 'afar on the unmeasured deep' as well as there being 'many other' continents. Aristotle (born 384 B.C.) mentions Antilla, Plutarch (born A.D. 46) refers to a continent called Saturnia; Marcelinus (born A.D. 330) wrote of the general belief in Atlantis and that 'a large island was swallowed up.' Proclus (born A.D. 410) recorded that inhabitants of Atlantic islands remembered a larger controlling one which had disappeared into the sea. Timagenes (born first century B.C.) refers to an 'island in the middle of the ocean' from which the Gauls claimed descent. Tertullian uses the sinking of Atlantis as an example of earth changes—observing that the island has been 'looked for in vain.' Some ancient accounts of such a lost continent do not, it must be said, meet the standards of complete credibility, such as the account by Theopompus of a discussion of a war-like outer continent between King Midas of Crete and Silenos, who, it is mentioned, was not only a satyr but also drunk at the time.

The most complete account we have concerning Atlantis is that of Plato (fifth century B.C.), who described it in two of his famous dialogues *Timaeus* and *Critias*. This account—studied and commented on for 2400 years—has given birth to a pro- and anti-Atlantis controversy which has lasted to the present day. It has been the subject of thousands of books, tens of thousands of articles, so that now the evocative word 'Atlantis' can hardly be mentioned in a discussion of prehistory without one's listeners being automatically divided into those who immediately classify Atlantis as a legend or a hoax and those who on hearing it have an instant vision of ancient grandeur, of an earthly paradise, of lost golden cities lying on the bottom of the ocean, of a continent sinking in a great cataclysm of nature, of survivors fleeing in ships to other parts of the world to preserve a culture which became our own.

Plato bases his account of Atlantis on what he said were actual written records kept by the Egyptian priests of Saïs, painted on temple columns. The priests explained these records to Solon, the Athenium lawgiver, an ancestor of Plato. Although he has been suspected of using an existing tradition as a 'vehicle' to make known his own themes of good government, the heroism of Athens in repelling an Atlantean invasion, and the end of Atlantis as the retribution of evil ... 'There occurred violent earthquakes and floods, and in a single day and night of rain all your warlike men in a body sunk into the earth, and the island of Atlantis in like manner disappeared, and was sunk beneath the sea. And that is the reason why the sea in those parts is impassable ...'

Within the dialogue Plato gave such exact descriptions of buildings, communication facilities, customs, people, history, topography, and distances that the dialogues seem to fill the function of an ancient 'travel guide' to Atlantis. In the intervening centuries and even today, some of his specific measurements are being checked against possible different locations for Atlantis, such as Crete, Thera, and scores of other sites, none of which are in the open Atlantic where Plato himself said Atlantis was. Some of his more inspiring passages indicated that *someone* had taken a good look at a powerful and highly developed civilization of ancient times.

After a description of the founding of Atlantis by Poseidon,

God of the Sea, he goes into detail about the wealth and splendor of an empire that reputedly extended as far as Egypt. ... 'They had such an amount of wealth as was never before possessed by kings and potentates, and is not likely ever to be again, and they were furnished with everything which they could have, both in city and country. For, because of the greatness of their empire, many things were brought to them from foreign countries, and the island itself provided much of what was required by them for the uses of life ... they dug out of the earth whatever was to be found there, mineral as well as metal, and that which is now only a name, and was then something more than a name—orichalcum—was dug out of the earth in many parts of the island, and, with the exception of gold, was esteemed the most precious of metals among the men of those days ...'

Plato makes a curious reference to elephants, which has suggested a connection with the legends and representations of elephants in America ... 'there were a great number of elephants in the island, and there was provision for animals of every kind, both for those which live in lakes and marshes and rivers, and also for those which live in mountains and on plains, and therefore for the animal which is the largest and most voracious of them ...'

His account of the climate of Atlantis and the variety of food found there represent an earthly paradise where living was without effort ... 'whatever fragrant things there are in the earth, whether roots, or herbage, or woods, or distilling drops of flowers or fruits, grew and thrived in that land, ... the cultivated fruit of the earth, both the dry edible fruit and other species of food ... and the fruits having a hard rind, affording drinks, and meats, and ointments, and good store of chestnuts and the like, which may be used to play with, and are fruits which spoil with keeping—and the pleasant kinds of dessert which console us after dinner, when we are full and tired of eating—all these that sacred island lying beneath the sea brought forth fair and wondrous in infinite abundance ...'

The description of construction work and huge palaces reminds one of cyclopean structures in other parts of the world

... 'They bridged over the zones of sea which surrounded the ancient metropolis, and made a passage into and out of the royal palace; and then they began to build the palace in the habitation of the god and of their ancestors ... beginning from the sea, they dug a canal three hundred feet in width and one hundred feet in depth, and fifty stadia in length, which they carried through to the outermost zone, making a passage from the sea up to this, which became a harbor, and leaving an opening sufficient to enable the largest vessels to find ingress. Moreover, they divided the zones of land which parted the zones of sea, constructing bridges of such a width as would leave a passage for a single trireme to pass out of one and into another, and roofed them over; and there was a way underneath for the ships, for the banks of the zones were raised considerably above the water ... The island in which the palace was situated had a diameter of five stadia. This, and the zones and the bridge, which was a sixth part of a stadium in width, they surrounded by a stone wall, on either side placing towers, and gates on the bridge where the sea passed in ...'

In mentioning the color of the stone of Atlantis, Plato unknowingly gave the same predominant colour of stones still existing on an Atlantic archipelago—the Canaries. In addition, Quetzalcóatl, the bearded white teacher who brought writing and other arts to ancient Mexico, is coincidently referred to as coming from 'the black and red land.' Plato said '... the stone which was used in the work they quarried from underneath the center island and from underneath the zones, on the outer as well as the inner side. One kind of stone was white, another black, and a third red; and, as they quarried, they at the same time hollowed out docks double within, having roofs formed out of the native rock. Some of their buildings were simple, but in others they put together different stones, which they intermingled for the sake of ornament, to be a natural source of delight ...'

Plato's persistent mention of gold and riches have been interpreted as referring to a link with the gold-rich ancient civilization of America, or the mysterious vanished culture of south-western Spain, Tartessos—the Tarshish of the Old Testament. Plato's work was familiar to Spaniards at the time of Columbus, who were bemused and fired by the prospect of unlimited gold ... 'The entire circuit of the wall which went round the outermost one they covered with a coating of brass, and the circuit of the next wall they coated with tin, and the third, which encompassed the citadel, flashed with the red light of orichalcum ... In the center was a holy temple dedicated to Cleito and Poseidon, which remained inaccessible, and was surrounded by an enclosure of gold ... All the outside of the temple, with the exception of the pinnacles, they covered with silver, and the pinnacles with gold. In the interior of the temple the roof was of ivory, adorned everywhere with gold and silver and orichalcum; all the other parts of the walls and pillars and floor they lined with orichalcum. In the temple they placed statues of gold: there was the god himself standing in a chariot—the charioteer of six winged horses—and of such size that he touched the roof of the building with his head; around him were a hundred Nereids riding on dolphins, for such was thought to be the number of them in that day ... And around the temple on the outside were placed statues of gold of all the ten kings and of their wives ...'

When Plato mentioned cold and hot springs for thermal bathing he correctly assessed an Atlantic island phenomenon —today in Reykjavik, Iceland, houses are heated and hot water is supplied from hot springs and hot volcanic springs are prevalent in the Azores, thought by some to be the mountaintops of Atlantis ... 'In the next place, they used fountains both of cold and hot springs; these were very abundant, and both kinds wonderfully adapted to use by reason of the sweetness and excellence of their waters. They constructed buildings about them, and placed suitable trees; also cisterns, some open to the heaven, others which they roofed over, to be used in winter as warm baths; there were the king's baths, and the baths of private persons, which were kept apart; also separate baths for women, and others again for horses and cattle, and to them they gave as much adornment as was suitable for them...'

A reference to irrigation reminds one of the enormous pre-Columbian irrigation schemes of South American coasts and plateaus... 'The water which ran off they carried, some to the grove of Poseidon, where were growing all manner of trees of wonderful height and beauty, owing to the excellence of the soil...'

In describing the commerce of the port, Plato has been suspected of using Tyre or other Phoenician or Cretan cities as models, in the unlikelihood of there being ocean commerce so long ago in the past. However, there seems to be an insistent connection between the secretive Phoenicians and the Western Ocean—perhaps going much farther back in time than we have suspected. 'The docks were full of triremes and naval stores, and all things were quite ready for use ... Crossing the outer harbors, which were three in number, you would come to a wall which began at the sea and went all round: this was everywhere distant fifty stadia from the largest zone and harbor, and enclosed the whole, meeting at the mouth of the channel toward the sea. The entire area was densely crowded with habitations; and the canal and the largest of the harbors were full of vessels and merchants coming from all parts, who, from their numbers, kept up a multitudinous sound of human voices and din of all sorts night and day...'

His descriptions of inner canals and irrigation remind one of the canal irrigation system of Mesopotamia and coastal Peru ... 'I will now describe the plain, which had been cultivated during many ages by many generations of kings. It was rectangular, and for the most part straight and oblong; and ... followed the line of the circular ditch. The depth and width and length of this ditch were incredible, and gave the impression that such a work, in addition to so many other works, could hardly have been wrought by the hand of man. But I must say what I have heard. It was excavated to the depth of a hundred feet, and its breadth was a stadium everywhere; it was carried round the whole of the plain, and was ten thousand stadia in length. It received the streams which came down from the mountains, and winding round the plain, and touching the city at various points, was then let off into the sea. From above, likewise, straight canals of a hundred feet in width were cut in the plain, and again let off into the ditch, toward the sea; these canals were at intervals of a hundred stadia, and by them they brought down the wood from the mountains to the city, and conveyed the fruit of the earth in ships, cutting transverse passages from one canal into another, and to the city. Twice in the year they gathered the fruits of the earth—in winter having the benefit of the rains, and in summer introducing the water of the canals ...'

Plato even gives an approximate figure for the number of military levies, also considered doubtful by critics as to the number of men and the use of horses, not shown to be domesticated until thousands of years later, unless the 9000-year figure for the sinking of Atlantis before the time of Plato is incorrect, or horses were domesticated at an earlier date than previously supposed ... 'The leader (of each section) was required to furnish for the war the sixth portion of a war chariot, so as to make up a total of ten thousand chariots; also two horses and riders upon them, and a light chariot without a seat, accompanied by a fighting man on foot carrying a small shield, and having a charioteer mounted to guard the horses; also, he was bound to furnish two heavy-armed men, two archers, two slingers, three stone-shooters, and three javelin men, who were skirmishers, and four sailors to make up a compliment of twelve hundred ships. Such was the order of war in the royal city—that of the other nine governments was different in each of them ...'

A connection with Crete and other islands of the Mediterranean is identifiable with the bull hunt and sacrifice—a ceremony which still links the Hispanic nations with the ancient past. 'There were bulls who had the range of the temple of Poseidon; and the ten [kings] who were left alone in the temple, after they had offered prayers to the gods that they might take the sacrifices which were acceptable to them, hunted the bulls without weapons, but with staves and nooses; and the bull which they caught they led up to the column; the victim was then struck on the head by them, and slain

111

over the sacred inscription ...' (The number of ten in Plato's account refers to the ten kings of Atlantis who were reputed to elect one of their number at intervals to rule over the others, a legend having an historical counterpart in the ten kings of the Mayas and the ten kings of the Canary Islands.)

The descriptive elements of Plato's account finds unusual parallels in the ancient Mediterranean and even in prehistoric America, and may represent a synthesis of Atlantic and Mediterranean legends or it may even be fairly factual. However, his account has been considered by many critics as either a pure fabrication or a storytelling device ever since he wrote it, and even his own later estranged pupil, Aristotle, commenting on Plato's sudden breaking off of the Atlantean dialogues, is said to have remarked: 'He who invented it (Atlantis), killed it.' A modern commentator and critic, Stephen Gsell, has attempted a final *coup de grâce*, observing 'Atlantis is mentioned only by Plato and those who have read him.'

Both were wrong. Atlantis was not 'invented' by Plato, but suggested by a shared memory of an Atlantic continent called Atlantis or other names we may never learn, by peoples and tribes living on the littoral of *both sides* of the Atlantic; in the east in what is now Ireland, Wales, France, Spain, Portugal, Morocco, and islands in the Mediterranean Sea and the Atlantic Ocean and, in the west, among the Indian tribes of what is now the United States, Mexico, Central and South America.

Among the myriad 'proofs' advanced for the existence or non-existence of Atlantis a rather nebulous one is perhaps the most convincing. It is the name Atlantis itself which is like a key that almost fits the lock to open the door to past ages. For we find that among many very ancient races, around the Atlantic coast, usually those sharing concepts of cyclopean structures, tools, inventions, medical knowledge, sun worship, mummification, and common customs and legends, the name of a vanished land in the ocean, or paradise, or the land of the dead, had a similar sound to the key vowels and consonants of the word 'Atlantis'—the letters A–T–L–N.

Plato used the word 'Atlantis' meaning the daughter or the

The Piri Reis map, dated 1513 but compiled from world maps of ancient times. The bottom of the map indicates land areas of the Antarctic continent apparently drawn when Antarctica was relatively free of ice. Correlation of points of longitude on this and other ancient maps indicate that some peoples of pre-history had a means of establishing longitude, enabling them to undertake sea voyages throughout the world.

Gold artifact from Columbian tomb over a thousand years old. Previously thought to be a bird, butterfly or fish, it was later noted to have the attributes of new models of delta wing jet fighter aircraft, especially the Swedish SAAB. *(Photo: J. A. Ulrich)*

Ceramic composite of elephant head, human face and foot from Cuenca. (Crespi Collection. Photo: J. Manson Valentine)

Stone tablets inscribed with elephants, sun symbols, pyramid and burial. (Crespi Collection. Photo: J. Manson Valentine)

Pre-Columbian incised stone found during construction of airport at Cuenca, Ecuador, showing elephants and symbols which may be writing. (Crespi Collection. Photo: J. Manson Valentine)

Gold headpiece with grid writing or symbols, Cuenca, Ecuador. (Crespi Collection. Photo: J. Manson Valentine)

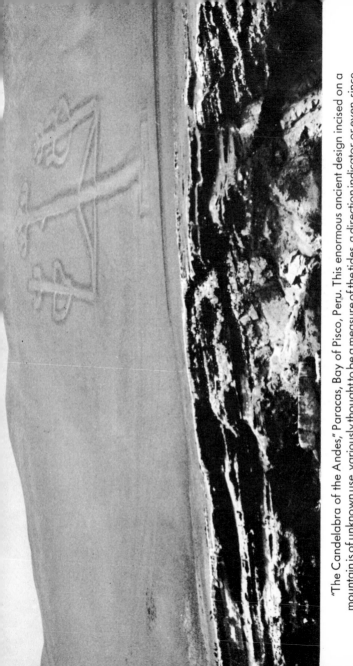

"The Candelabra of the Andes," Paracas, Bay of Pisco, Peru. This enormous ancient design incised on a mountain is of unknown use, variously thought to be a measure of the tides, a direction indicator, or even, since ropes were originally found attached to the arms, a gigantic seismograph for measuring earthquakes. (Photo: J. Manson Valentine)

The Great Pyramid, Gizeh, Egypt. As former limestone facing has been removed, through the ages, for buildings in Cairo, true measurements involving the pyramidal inch had to be calculated allowing for thickness of limestone covering. (Photo courtesy of United Arab Republic Tourist Office)

El Panecillo, Quito, Ecuador. The city of Quito is seen in the centre of the photograph, with the small mountain, El Panecillo, to the right. This mountain has long been considered a natural formation, but recent investigations suggest that it is a man-made mound, raised in remote antiquity. (Photo: Bodo Wuth)

Fitted stones in wall at Sacsahuaman, Peru. It is not known how the pre-Incas could have transported such enormous stones nor could have cut them to fit so exactly, not only on the surface, but also in depth, and finally, why they were set at such odd angles – perhaps for economy of cutting or to prevail against earthquakes. (Photo: J. Manson Valentine)

Machu Picchu, Peru. This "lost" city built on a mountaintop at an elevation of 6850 feet, 1000 feet straight up from the Urubamba river gorge, was not rediscovered until 1912. Other lost temples, forts and cities are reputed to exist in parts of the Andes or the jungle regions to the east. *(Photo courtesy of Pan American World Airways, Inc.)*

Terraces at Machu Picchu. Some of these terraces were used for growing crops at an amazing altitude for agriculture. Many instances of incredibly high stone terraces exist in different mountain sections of South America, some reaching up to the permanent snow line of the Andes. *(Photo courtesy of Pan American World Airways Inc.)*

Aerial view of the underwater Bimini road or wall. This unusual picture was taken from a few inches below the surface of the water by means of a special technique developed by Dimitri Rebikoff, somewhat analogous in underwater photography, to aerial survey in order to afford a consecutive photo-study of the placement of underwater cyclopean stone.

Diver John Gifford on bottom examining section between rocks to determine possible use of mortar, or tool marks, or another layer of slabs under the rocks. The size and fitting of the rocks resembles to some extent other monolithic structures in different parts of the world, especially in Peru. (Photo: Dimitri Rebikoff)

Divers seen to the left on the facing page and in the centre above are on the bottom seen from the top of the water at a depth of 3 to 4 fathoms. The complete wall or road is calculated to be about 1600 feet long, with indications that it may go much further, and is composed of blocks of limestone 15 to 20 feet square. *(Photo: Dimitri Rebikoff)*

Divers photographing the "Bimini Wall." To the right of the photograph can be seen a gulley which generally separates the two formations which, according to some opinion, may have formed when the wall or stone pier cracked in a seismic disturbance. *(Photo: Dimitri Rebikoff)*

The Temple of the Turtles, Uxmal, Yucatán. The plan of his historic Maya temple is basically similar to the underwater stone building foundation found at Andros in 1968. (Photo: J. Manson Valentine)

Mount Pico in the Azores Islands. The Azores as well as the Canary and Madeira Islands have long been considered by Antlantologists to be vestiges of Atlantis – the mountain tops of the lost continent rising from the plains and river valleys which are now beneath the sea. *(Photo: José Goulart – Courtesy of Portuguese Information and Tourist Office)*

Area of the "Seven Cities," São Miguel, the Azores. Legends of the Azores contain many references to the lost continent and violent seismic disturbances some of which in effect are still continuing along the length of the Mid-Atlantic Ridge, one of the world's principal earthquake zones. *(Photo courtesy of Regional Commission of Tourism in the Azores)*

Incised carving on stone found on the slopes of the Sierra Nevada de Santa Marta, Colombia. The megalithic carvings indicate great age and depth but their meaning remains unknown. Enormous carved rocks have also been found in the Amazon and Orinoco River tributary systems, many of which contain writing, either Phoenician, other Mediterranean languages, or unknown scripts. *(Photo: J. Manson Valentine)*

The mysterious giant spheres of unknown age, originally found in the jungles of Costa Rica and more recently in Mexico, Aruba, and Haiti, are so exactly round that it has been suggested that they are natural formations, although some of them show traces of tool marks. According to one theory they are representations of planets and moons of the solar system or systems and, if they had been left where they were originally placed, would form a gigantic prehistoric planetarium. *(Photo courtesy of Carlos M. Peralta)*

Temple platform at Tula, Mexico. Tula is thought to be the archaeological site identified with Quetzalcóatl and the Toltec civilisation of
ancient Mexico linked through legend with the mythical lost land of
Aztlán or Tlapallan in the Eastern (Atlantic) Ocean. Of special
interest are "Atlantean" columns which supported a now vanished
roof reminiscent of construction techniques of the ancient Mediterranean. *(Photo courtesy of Mexican Government Tourist Department)*

Olmec head excavated in San Lorenzo, Mexico, when small part of right forehead was noticed under burned over jungle. These enormous heads, in appearance more African than Indian, are one of the New World's greatest and oldest mysteries. *(Photo: Dr. Gordon Ekholm, Courtesy of American Museum of Natural History)*

land of Atlas (the legendary giant who held up the sky). Atlas is the name of the range of mountains in Northwest Africa whose peaks continue out under the Atlantic Ocean, reappearing over the surface as the Canary Islands. In the Canary Islands themselves the name reappeared as the megalithic cavern complex of Atalaya. When the inhabitants of the Canary Islands were still in contact with the Roman world they were said to be survivors of a lost continent. Certain tribes of western North Africa were called the Atarantes and the Atlantioi, and classical writers frequently referred to the inhabitants of Spain as Atlanteans.

In the middle of the Atlantic Ocean, the Carthaginians and their predecessors, the Phoenicians, apparently had visited a great island called Antilla, which often appears on medieval maps and may represent the Azores or Atlantis itself. It is highly probable that Columbus, on his first voyage, carried with him a copy of the Benicasa Map, which showed Antilla or Antilha in the middle of the Atlantic Ocean as the Azores had already been discovered and marked.

Across the ocean to the New World, we find that the ancient Aztecs told the Spanish conquistadors that their ancestors, the people of Az, came from Aztlán, a sunken land in the east and that the 'fair god' Quetzalcóatl, a white-bearded teacher, had also come from a land in the sea called Tollán-Tlallapan. Another linguistic coincidence appears when we consider that the Aztec word for 'water'—*atl*—also means 'water' in Berber, the language of a non-Arabic people inhabiting the Atlas Mountains of North Africa.

The Mayas, also of Central America, kept this tradition of a white god, called Kukulkán, who brought civilization. They also remembered the land of Aztlán, as did the Venezuelan 'white' Indians (who disappeared soon after the Spanish conquest), who had a settlement called Atlán after the vanished island. If we continue back to Europe, we recognize the sound in the misty lost Avallon of the Welsh, and perhaps even in the Germanic Valhalla, the warriors' paradise of fighting and drinking. Returning to what we have long considered the oldest civilization, we find the Egyptian Land of the Dead, located in the west, and called Aalu or Amenti, while the Babylonian paradise is Arallu. In Suras VII, XXVI, XLI, XLVI, and LXXXIX of the Koran, the Bible of Islam, part of which contains references from older writings, the first syllable of the name of the lost continent is almost recognizable in the mention of the people of Ad, an advanced race who built the City of Pillars, and who were punished by God for their wickedness, as were the last of the generations before Noah, in the Great Flood, whose memory occurs in almost all races of the world. But, besides the flood mentioned in the Old Testament, there seems to be no mention of the linking name, unless the name of the first man may have meant the collective name of the first great civilized race, like the people of Ad— 'Ad-am.'

The various interpretations of a name, the common points of custom, shared mythology, ancient references, identical legends and stories, similar architecture and knowledge are thought-provoking but offer no positive proof of Atlantis acceptable to the cold eye of scientific discipline.

The unexplained presence of continental animal and insect life in the Azores, the Canaries and Madeira implies that the Azores was once part of a continent or land bridge. This applies to the monk seal of the Azores, a species that generally lives along coastlines or archipelagoes; the rabbits found on the Azores; the indigenous dogs of the Canary Islands (from which the islands got their present name); the same genus of earthworms existing in Europe, North Africa and the Atlantic Islands; butterflies and beetles common to America and Africa; a fresh-water mollusk common to Europe and America and also to the Azores: the Cypraea mollusks, common to the Azores, the Canaries, the west coast of Africa *and* the east coast of the United States, whose sensitive larvae do not persist in deep water; and small crustaceans in the Canary Islands, of which blind members of the species live in underwater caves (while non-blind members of the same species live in the ocean waters) as if the former had been trapped by a sudden cataclysm in the lightless cave waters.

In order to explain the presence not only of small animals

114

common to Europe and the New World but also of larger ones, such as the extinct mastodons, elephants, and horses as well as the indigenous human population, it has often been suggested that land bridges still linked the two hemispheres in Pleistocene and Pliocene times, inasmuch as the continental drift—the Wegener theory of continents drifting apart—would be too slow a rate—several centimeters a year—to account for the presence of some forms of advanced animal life. Concerning land bridges instead of once extant continents one is reminded of Charles Hapgood's observation: '...Land bridges have been very convenient for many scientists seeking to avoid the horrid alternative of former continents.'

Animals, however, do not indicate the presence of an advanced civilization, and even the contemporaneous report that the Guanches, the indigenous Canary Islanders, who still had ten elective kings, like Plato's report of Atlantis, when they were rediscovered by Spanish navigators in the fourteenth century expressed surprise that the Spaniards had survived the universal sinking of their former continent, is not conclusive, as it is simply another oral tradition kept by them *after they had forgotten* their written language.

The Canary Islands, where an ancient survival race was found (and exterminated) and the Azores where statues, plaques, and underwater ruins have been reportedly found are considered by some researchers to be the mountain peaks of the sunken Atlantean continent.

Modern interest in Atlantis occurs in recurrent waves, like the waves of the ocean breaking on a beach. And with the increasing interest of the present generation and the development of underwater exploration and discoveries we may be approaching the cumulative or seventh wave which occurs in a series of breakers.

The thousands of books written to prove or disprove the existence of Atlantis in the mid-Atlantic (or a wide variety of other locations) have missed the most logical explanation of all, one closely connected with the underwater finds in the Bahamas and the Caribbean and one basically acceptable even to the archaeological 'establishment.' The odd thing about it is that it has been so evident—perhaps that is why it was not realized. It is simply this: the Bahama Banks are known to have been above water during the last glaciation, as were large parts of the continental shelf all over the world. The Hudson River in New York continues in canyons that go far out to sea, as do the Atlantis river canyons of French and Spanish rivers, the La Plata in Argentina and other ocean emptying rivers. Such canyons cannot be cut underwater. Nor does beach sand form deep on the bottom of the ocean, as in the case of the submerged beaches of the Azores.

To 'solve' one aspect of the Atlantis controversy, therefore, we must ask only: Did the water level rise greatly at a time at the edge of recorded history? This time we get the answer from geologists and glacier specialists—a satisfactory 'Yes'—with the accelerated melting of the last glaciers perhaps 12,000 years ago. This represented a rise of about 600 feet, covering the coastal plains of continents *and islands* and covering, if they existed, roads, walls, cities of the pre-flood peoples, the survivors of which would preserve an unforgettable legend of the rising waters, floods, and rain which overwhelmed them.

Ocean depths have been variously calculated at different periods, more exactly since the echo sounder in 1920, later with sonar, and even more accurately since 1950 with the Precision Depth Recorder. With the fairly complete soundings that we now possess of the world's oceans we are able to construct a world picture of lands existing during the last glacial period that may provide a partial answer to the locations of early habitations of man and possible early civilizations.

We find such shallow depths in the North Sea, the English Channel, and in the sea bottom south and west of Ireland that we may assume them to have been dry land before the rise of the ocean waters, a supposition reinforced by the findings of ancient mastodon bones and Stone Age tools at the bottom of the North Sea, and of underwater constructions under investigation by divers working with Paster Spanuth off Heligoland. The west coasts of France and Ireland abound in legends of cities beneath the sea which, though partially attributed to

Celtic imagination and mysticism, have been borne out by certain neolithic underwater finds off the west coast of France. Some of the avenues of menhirs, the large standing stones, continue out under the Atlantic and their underwater continuation can be seen when unusually low tides occur every few years, at five- or ten-year intervals.

In the Mediterranean a lowered water level of hundreds of feet would have added a considerable land mass to the coastline east of Tunisia and would have joined Sicily to the Italian mainland as Roman writers have reported it to have been. The Greek islands would have been larger and considerably more numerous; they are, in fact, so shown on the Ibn Ben Zara map of Alexandria of 1487 which was, like the Piri Reis and other maps, copied from ancient charts made at a much earlier period, evidently detailing many islands in the Aegean Sea which are now under water. It is especially interesting to note, in view of the recent theories of Greek archaeologists such as Drs. Galanapoulos and Marianatos, that the Island of Thera, north of Crete, was Atlantis, or at least gave rise to the Atlantean 'legend'; that an island on the Ibn Ben Zara map, resembling Thera, is shown to be comparatively much larger at the time the map was made, possibly thousands of years ago. The present island of Thera is considered to have lost a great part of its area in a volcanic explosion of 1500 B.C. It has had many earthquakes since and is still 'smoking.'

A large part of the bottom of the Mediterranean, moreover, seems to consist of cliffs, crags, and valleys, as if it were not sea bottom but land covered by the sea. Many of the cities and ports of the Mediterranean now under water have been engulfed or sunk within historic times, sometimes even going down and then coming up again, as can be seen in the case of ancient temple columns in Pozzuoli, Italy, now above water, which show distinct marks of underwater borers from the temple's last prolonged immersion in the sea. However, there are other earlier sunken cities in the Mediterranean and the Aegean located at much greater depths, to which they may have fallen as the result of the many earthquakes endemic to the region.

117

Besides subsidence of known historical ports in the Mediterranean, much older and deeper undersea roads and buildings are now constantly being discoverd by free divers, often hunting for fish or for other objects. Enormous walls composed of blocks 8 meters long and 6 meters high, at a minimum depth of about 14 meters were found on the bottom in Moroccan waters on the Mediterranean side of Gibraltar by Marc Valentin in 1958, while free-diving in pursuit of a fish, and were eventually traced for a distance of several miles. The general construction of these walls, surrounded by smaller stones,

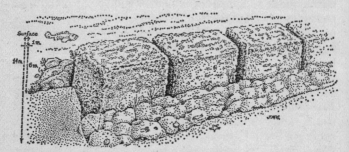

Sketch of wall found by spear fisherman on sea bottom off Morocco. A combination of large blocks and boulders, it is roughly estimated to run along the sea bottom for nine miles.

bears a striking resemblance to prehistoric cyclopean stonework on the coasts of the Atlantic and on the Mediterranean islands that are still above water. Further deep sinkings of prehistoric buildings and towns have been noted near Thera and especially near Melos where another free diver, Jim Thorne, in a series of dives connected with the possible retrieval of the arms of the Venus de Milo (in Greek nomenclature, the Aphrodite of Melos) inadvertently found a prehistoric sunken citadel at several hundred feet, from which other roads and pathways proceeded downward to even greater depths.

In the Americas we find a wide continental shelf extending from Newfoundland to Nova Scotia, where it is hundreds of miles wide, and then again from hundreds of miles east of Cape Cod all the way down to Florida, narrowing to an average of 90 to 100 miles out to sea, all well under the approximate 600-foot depth of a lower water level in glacial times. This underwater area, presumably once dry land, becomes greater through the Bahamas, off Yucatán and Central America and then again off the northern coast of South America, narrows in Brazil and extends hundreds of miles out from Rio de Janeiro southward.

The Atlantic Ocean is divided in the middle by a mountainous ridge or a series of mountain chains which run from Iceland down to the northeastern part of South America, then follows it east almost to Africa and continues due south. In the region of north latitude 38° west longitude 37° to 30°, on a more or less direct line from Lisbon, some of these mountain peaks break the surface of the Atlantic and become the Azores Islands, rising from the underwater Azores Plateau. One of the Azores Islands, Pico, is a huge mountain 24,000 feet high, of which 16,400 are underwater and another 7600 feet continue above sea level. (The precipitous peak of Pico reminds one of Plato's description of the great central mountain of the main island of Atlantis rising over the fertile Atlantean plain.)

For the last ninety years, there has been a tremendous resurgence of interest in the possibility of Atlantis having actually existed partially revived by thousands of books written on the subject, including the best-seller written by Ignatius Donnelly in 1882, *Atlantis—Myths of the Antediluvian World*, and still published in an edition updated by the United Kingdom's leading Atlantologist, Edgarton Sykes.

Although Atlantis has been 'located' in many parts of the world, considerably more than a third of sources that have researched the Atlantean 'problem' locate it in the sunken plateau around the Azores, possibly including the Madeira and Canary Islands (whose original inhabitants thought they were survivors of Atlantis), and other points beneath the sea. This is a conveniently placed location in that it is more or less where Plato indicated it was, as well as being the widest part of the Atlantic Ridge between the true sea bottom on the east of the Iberian Basin and on the west of the North American Basin and the Abyssal Plain. Moreover, since the perfection of underwater depth soundings, measurements have been taken which would have delighted Donnelly and other early investigators of Atlantis in the late nineteenth and early twentieth centuries. For, if we consider the immediate underwater plateau encompassing the Azores Islands, we find a submerged land mass with peninsulas, isthmuses and bays, underwater mountains and valleys that is larger than Portugal. The whole area is at a depth varying from 400 to 900 feet, most of which, as well as other islands nearby to the north and to the east along the Azores Rise, would have been above water 12,000 years ago. (We are reminded of what Plato said about islands by which one could sail to the true encompassing continent on the other side!) And, if we take the lower second stage of the Azores Plateau at an even greater depth of between 1000 and 2000 feet, we obtain measurements of a huge island or a small continent, still completely differentiated in topography from the surrounding abyssal plain of the true ocean.

Certain features of the present-day Azores and even some maritime customs of the present inhabitants give strong indications of sunken lands. Fishermen are in the habit of throwing over pails, at a determined spot far out in the ocean to the west of Flores, to obtain fresh drinking water from the ocean. A hundred miles to the west of the archipelago, fishermen know of a place where they can anchor their boats in what appears to be the middle of the ocean. Often when they throw their nets they are torn by jagged lava rocks where there should be deep sea bottom.

Parts of the Azores seem still to be disappearing into the sea. The islands of Flores and Corvo, when they were first settled by the Portuguese, were closer together, but now have lost so much land that the distance between them has increased. Constant volcanic action causes depth measurements of the ocean to be revised and this same volcanic action is doubtlessly the explanation of the hot and cold springs in the Azores (Plato again!) and some other unusual aqueous features including contiguous but separate blue and green lakes in São Miguel, an underwater lake in Graziosa, and a completely dry lake bed in Flores.

There are several startling evidences of extreme land sinking or subsidence: near the Azores cores containing fresh water algae have been taken from a depth of 12,000, which indicates that these algae once lived in a lake above sea level. Moreover, thousands of feet down under the ocean there are shelves covered with sand, although beach sand forms only where waves have broken for centuries on a land shoreline.

Rocks from the ocean bottom tend to confirm the submergence theory. In 1898 a cable ship attempting to retrieve an Atlantic cable that had broken north of the Azores, brought up pieces of tachylite, a kind of vitreous lava, formed only *above* water under atmospheric pressure and dated about 12,000–13,000 years old. More recently, on an expedition sponsored by the U.S.S.R. Academy of Science, Dr. Maria Klinova, examining rocks dredged up from the sea bottom 60 miles north of the Azores, at a depth of 6600 feet, found evidence of their being formed under atmospheric pressure and estimated their submergence at 15000 B.C. (Interest in Atlantis has increased in the U.S.S.R. along with interest in the world's oceans, fleets, and submarines, the latter, in the course of other activities, perhaps representing a potential aid in Atlantean Research.) Both of these widely separated discoveries place dated portions of the bottom of the Atlantic roughly within Plato's time frame for the sinking of Atlantis.

Fairly recent investigations by American scientists and oceanographers seem to corroborate the theory of submerging Atlantic lands. Professor Ewing of Columbia University found evidence that lava had spread only recently on the bottom of the ocean and stated: 'Either the land must have sunk two to three miles, or the sea once must have been two to three miles lower than now. Either conclusion is startling.' Professor Bruce Heezen, on a Duke University project over the Puerto Rico Trench, identified coral reefs at extreme depths and observed: 'Coral reefs don't grow in more than fifty feet of water. This means that the area we studied once had to be

121

near sea level.'

Within recent periods tremendous variations in ocean depths have been recorded in the same place as if the ocean bottom were constantly rising and falling. In 1923 a Western Union cable repair ship reported an apparent rise of two miles in the same area where a cable had been laid twenty-five years previously. Taking into account that soundings at that period were considerably less accurate than the improved techniques developed from 1950 on, we may expect more detailed and precise accounts in the future, as for example the reported rising of the floor of the Caribbean by extrusion of basalt rock of the 'continental' type on the sea bottom.

But did Atlantis really sink, or was it simply drowned by rising waters? Part of it could certainly have sunk, for the mid-Atlantic ridge is located on the world's most active earthquake belt, with constant undersea volcanic disturbances changing the depth and topography of the ocean bottom, alternately causing islands, through the centuries, to appear and disappear, or to become larger or smaller. Only recently a large island, Surtsey, rose out of the sea off Iceland, dramatically accompanied by volcanic explosions.

There are approximately 100,000 earthquakes every year, caused by shifting stress of the earth's crust along the 'lines of weakness.' Most of these earthquakes, of which about a thousand are serious, take place under the sea, along the great earthquake fault which goes down the centre of the Atlantic, partially east to the Mediterranean, with flares continuing to Central Asia, but principally around Africa into the Great Rift Valley of Africa, into the Indian Ocean, continuing south of Australia, then through the Pacific north to Indonesia, Japan, the Aleutians, Alaska, and California, and also southeast to Mexico, Chile, and Peru. For untold centuries one of the chief, if not the principal, earthquake area of the world has been the Atlantic Ridge on the bottom of the Atlantic, precisely where the reputed eighth continent—Atlantis—is said to have sunk into the ocean which now bears its name.

If we examine the Pacific Ocean we find that it has no great central ridge like the Atlantic. The Pacific is considered to be

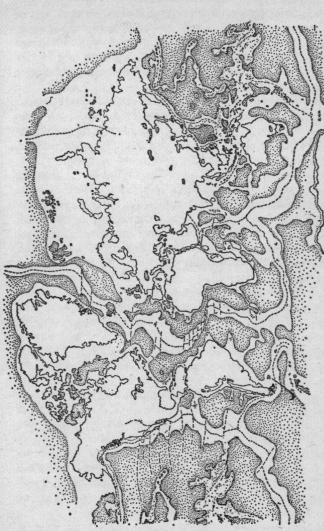

Principal earthquake fracture zones throughout the world, showing area of great tectonic activity along the Atlantic Ridge. White dotted areas through the oceans indicate path of fracture zone.

the original great ocean of the earth—the *Panthalassa*—the all-encompassing sea, on which, according to the Wegener theory of continental drift, the original land mass of the earth formed, split into continental sections, which drifted apart like huge floating islands, forming the present continents and islands which are still drifting at leisurely rates of several centimeters or more a year.

The underwater ranges of this residual super-sea do not form, except close to the continental land masses, any considerable sunken lands to indicate that an extra continent may once have been above sea level during the Holocene era, the Age of Man. Underwater mountain chains, some of which run east to west, occasionally break the surface in the form of series of islands like the Caroline, Mariana, Marshall, Gilbert, and Hawaiian Island chains, the Aleutians in the north and the Melanesian groups in the south. However, if the water level were calculated at 600 feet lower in the glacial era, some of these islands, such as the Hawaiian Islands, would connect on dry land. Moreover, Australia would have had land connected to Southeast Asia and large portions of the sea bottoms in Indonesia and Malaysia would be land.

Cyclopean ruins found on Pacific islands, of which the present inhabitants conserve only vague legends, has given rise to popular speculation that such islands must be the vestigial remains of another lost continent. Such a continental land mass must have existed, it is reasoned, to explain the hundreds of cyclopean statues and structures on Easter Island, whose present area would support only a small population; the huge stone city on Ponape in the Carolines; stone ruins and roads running into the sea on other islands and legends of a great empire in the Pacific. Memories of this empire have persisted down to modern times as demonstrated by the tribute payments involving Yap, Truk, and other islands whereby islanders would deliver tribute to far-off points without knowing exactly why, except that it would be tabu *not* to do so.

Unlike Atlantis, this projected Pacific lost continent has an element of confusion in its name, Mu or Lemuria. The name

Lemuria originally was suggested by biologists for a hypothetical continent in the Indian Ocean which would explain the presence of lemurs and other fauna found only on Madagascar, but has been borrowed by the supporters of the theory of a lost continent in the Pacific. The word Mu was first brought to public attention by the mistranslation of Maya records by the French 'Americanists,' or researchers of American Indian civilization, Le Plongeon and Brasseur de Bourbourg in the nineteenth century.

The location of a single continent in the immense Pacific Ocean is doubtful. Some of the archaeological mysteries which dot the various islands are separated by thousands of miles. The deserted city of Nan Madol in the Carolines is almost the Pacific's width away from the mysterious archaeological zone of Rapa Nui, or Easter Island, which is so far to the east that it lies almost due south of Gallup, New Mexico. Other ruins, stone roads and docks, truncation of mountaintops to form plateaus, rock carvings and picture writing exist in such widely separated places as Hawaii, Pitcairn, Yap, Malden, in the Line Islands, and the Marquesas.

The deserted city of uncertain date on Ponape whose size and construction gives evidence of a former powerful and well organized culture that has vanished almost without echoes, Nan Madol, also called Metalanim (or Meteranimu during the long Japanese rule of the Carolines), covers over eleven square miles, crisscrossed by canals and constructed of huge, perfectly cut basalt blocks, transported from quarries 30 miles distant. Some of its walls are 40 feet high and 18 feet thick. A most unusual feature of its construction is that its canals apparently were built up instead of down, and the islands themselves are largely artificial, being actually stone platforms laid in the ocean. Stone was laid on the top of the coral reefs to form a series of connected islands and canals. Huge breakwaters to protect the city were laid in the ocean itself and a sea gate permitted the great canoes access to the sea.

The amount of man-power necessary to build such a city and its suggestion of a former land area now submerged is commented on by J. Macmillan Brown in *The Riddle of the*

Pacific: 'The rafting over the reef at high tide and the hauling up of these immense blocks, many of them from five to twenty-five tons in weight, to such height as sixty feet must have meant tens of thousands of organized labour; and it had to be housed and clothed and fed. Yet within a radius of fifteen hundred miles from this as a center there are not more than fifty thousand people today. It is one of the miracles of the Pacific unless we assume a subsidence of twenty times as much land as now exists...'

Native legends concerning the building of the city are considerably lacking in technical details—god-like heroes were supposed to have made the stones fly from the distant quarries into their positions in the walls, canals, and breakwaters, a similar explanation given for the cyclopean buildings in the Andes. A concentrated population, well organized and provided with sophisticated tools and techniques would, of course, have been able to build Nan Madol and the enigmatic constructions on other Pacific islands.

Most of these islands had much greater populations when they were first discovered by white men than subsequently, when disease, alcohol, slavery, and sometimes outright slaughter had decimated the population. In general, however, what were apparently once relatively well-developed civilizations were in a state of cultural retreat at the time they were discovered; again strangely paralleling the case of Indian America, where, as in the Pacific, legends of former greater races were retained.

It may be that the tremendous artifacts of Ponape, Rapa Nui, and other islands were not built as part of a culture of an extensive 'lost continent' but constructed by descendants of races that had been influenced, conquered, or taught by members of a great seafaring race that had since vanished, either through racial absorption or some other reason. Indications that cultural development stopped with alarming suddenness in some Pacific islands are prevalent in legends of destruction and sudden catastrophe. Even the ruins show traces of sudden interruption. Scores of the Easter Island statues were still being worked on when something caused the carvers to drop their tools. Dressed stone blocks were stacked awaiting shipment and at Nan Madol some of the cyclopean walls under construction were never completed.

Volcanic eruptions may have caused considerable land changes in the undersea ranges whose mountain peaks are the Pacific islands. Easter Island, for example, is situated on a high cone rising from the ocean floor at the Nasca Plateau, and is located on a most unstable base, between three 'fracture zones'—the Easter Island fracture zone to the north and the Challenger and Méndez fracture zones to the south.

The Pacific, like the Atlantic, is characterized by a profusion of 'sea-mounts'—mysterious cones rising from the bottom but with flattened tops, sometimes fairly close to the surface. It has been suggested that these sea-mounts were once islands, the flat surfaces of which were formerly above water at some time in the past. Conversely, in both oceans, we find former beaches raised to great heights on land; 400 feet at Paracas, Peru; 1300 feet near Valparaiso, Chile; 1500 feet in northern California and 1700 feet on the coast of Greenland. That such changes took place during periods of civilization is evidenced by the fact that artifacts—bits of fish nets, potsherds, and woven cloth have been found in the 'cross-bedding' of sand, shells, and earth thrown up hundreds of feet in the form of the raised beaches of Peru. If former beaches could be raised to such a height it might be logically assumed that other lands could be depressed in a compensatory reaction.

Considering the enormous diffusion of prehistoric Pacific culture and the ability of navigators to find distant relatively small islands while traveling for long periods out of sight of land, one has the feeling that the early Pacific navigators had once had access to techniques and information from a previous advanced age of navigation, when early but far from primitive seafarers sailed all over a younger world, mapped its oceans and charted its skies.

Some unusual and unexpected items of knowledge, developed by the Pacific islanders or inherited by them, tend to indicate, like their amazing ruins, ties to a more sophisticated culture. Somehow the early navigators, in their great double canoes, were able to navigate great distances over the Pacific at an earlier date and on voyages of greater length than that made by Columbus—voyages of weeks and months. As far as we know they had certain navigational aids made of wood that were coordinated to star positions, perhaps a legacy from another earlier seafaring people. The voyage of the Hawaiians from Tahiti to Hawaii is but one example of their navigational expertise. The Maoris, who migrated a thousand years ago en masse from Polynesia to New Zealand, knew not only a great deal about the positions of the stars but also, in some fashion, were aware that the planet Saturn had rings. In archaeological investigations at Easter Island three cultural levels have been established, the oldest being the most advanced. Stone carvings on rocks at Easter Island show an ancient ship with three masts, larger and different from those used by the inhabitants when they were discovered.

Many of the Polynesian tabus or things that must not be done or must not be neglected under threat of gods' or ghosts' displeasure as well as the incantations of magicians may be additional vestiges of ancient medical knowledge disguised as magic. In a comprehensive book on Ponape, Sibley S. Morill gives a well-substantiated opinion that Ponapean 'medicine men' possess an effective cure for tetanus and gonorrhea as well as 'potions' for relieving heart attacks and stopping pregnancy.

An outstanding example of cultural regression among the peoples of the Pacific islands is the loss of the Easter Island system of writing before it could be translated. When Easter Island was first visited some of the islanders, in a population of perhaps 6000, could still read the mysterious *rongo-rongo* writings, written or carved on flat boards and also carved on rocks. The writing seems to be a syllabic alphabet, some of the characters representing human figures and others line figures of simple design. After the depredations of slavery and disease, when the population was reduced to about one hundred survivors, everyone who once could read had died off and with them the secret of the 'alphabet' and the contents of the

128

records. Other similar writing, equally undecipherable, has been found in the Caroline Islands.

The Easter Island alphabet, or syllabary, as it is thought to be, for it has over five hundred signs, presents another mystery equal to or greater than the Easter Island statues themselves. It is apparently related to the writing of a vanished culture completely on the other side of the world, about as far from Easter Island as one could possibly get on the earth's surface. For, if a line were pierced through the axis of the earth, entering at Easter Island and emerging at a point diametrically opposite, it would come out in the vicinity of the Indus Valley, Pakistan, site of the great cities of Mohenjo-Daro and Harappa, thought to be as old as 4500 years and to predate the historical culture of India. This Indus Valley culture extended the length and breadth of the Indus Valley and included enormous well-planned and populous brick cities with sophisticated water, sewerage, and waste disposal systems. It ended in sudden conquest and ruin by invaders from the north in about 1500 B.C. so suddenly that skeletons of the slaughtered inhabitants have been found preserved at the old street level.

The Indus Valley culture is thought to be contemporaneous with ancient Sumeria, the script of which we can read, but the writing of Mohenjo-Daro and Harappa has proved indecipherable, since the language itself has disappeared, along with the people who spoke it.

The maximum possible earthly distance between the Indus Valley and Easter Island makes all the more incredible the fact that many of the letters or syllables of the surviving script, written in the Indus Valley on seals for signatures, stamping, or identification, and on Easter Island on the 'speaking woods' (the *rongo-rongo* boards) or carved on rocks, are so identical as to make chance or coincidental resemblance inconceivable. The resemblance is so close that, taking into consideration that the Easter Island script often has a double line, we can project from an Indus Valley sign what is Easter Island counterpart will be.

The Easter Island script was in use until fairly recent times and some of the wooden tablets escaped the predictable destruction caused by missionaries. One memorized line was identified by Bishop Jaussen of Tahiti through an Easter Island survivor living in Tahiti. The former Easter Islander had apparently memorized the content of a tablet, but could no longer separate the sound except that he consistently

Examples of ancient scripts of Easter Island (top) and Indus Valley (bottom) compared. These two scripts, both 'unbroken,' have been found in diametrically opposite points of the earth's surface, each being one half of the world's diameter away from the other. Intervening or connecting scripts have not yet been discovered.

pointed to one phrase containing the same symbols, translating them as 'They addressed their prayers to the god of Rangitea.' If the translation is correct, this serves to compound the mystery, as Rangitea lies in the Friendly Islands, across 1500 miles of open ocean.

The existence of a script isolated on an island thousands of miles from any land in the world's largest ocean, halfway around the world from a similar script of prehistoric West India implies not only a common origin, but a diffusion of culture, and is a fairly concrete indication of unrecorded early sea voyages of a range and scope previously considered impossible.

However, if the sea level had been lower, or land masses somewhat differently arranged, such voyages, while still long, would have been feasible, and would thereby facilitate cultural, racial, and linguistic diffusion on coastal lands throughout the world.

CHAPTER EIGHT

THE GODS FROM THE SEA

Most anthropologists accept the theory that the ancestors of the American Indians once walked from Siberia over the then frozen Bering Straits and eventually populated the Americas from Alaska to the southern tip of Tierra del Fuego with the wild tribes and civilized empires and nations found in America by the first European explorers. Everyone seems to believe this except the Indians themselves, past and present, who have conserved oral, written, and pictorial traditions of their provenance, practically none of which have to do with Siberia.

The Aztecs of Mexico, the Toltecs, who preceded them, the Maya, and other tribes of central America trace their origin to an island in the eastern sea named Aztlán or Atlán (to the eternal satisfaction of proponents of the Atlantean tradition). They even describe, in documents recorded after the Spanish conquests, when the tradition was still fresh, where the original ancestors landed on the Mexican coast (near Vera Cruz) and how they brought their treasured books and paintings with them. Bishop Landa, the enigmatical instigator of the destruction of Maya records, and later student of what remained recorded at a time close to the original conquest of Yucatán that in Yucatán the traditions all point to an *eastern and foreign* origin for the race. The only transcribers of Maya records reported that 'The natives believe their ancestors to have *crossed the sea* by a passage which was opened for them.' The Quiché Maya of Guatemala record in their chronicle, the *Popul Vuh*: 'The three sons of the Quiché King made a visit to the land situated to the east, from which our ancestors came.'

Among the Indians of the United States there is a widespread tradition of immigration, usually by sea, from the East. The Indians of the Great Lakes believed that their progenitors once dwelt 'toward the rising sun.' Hopi traditions trace their wanderings from the tropical south and recount that they once escaped destruction by living under the sea, while other survivors escaped the drowning of the 'Third World' by crossing the sea on huge reed rafts. The Leni-Lenapi Indians of Delaware believed that they came from 'the first land ... beyond the great ocean' and, according to Sioux tradition: 'The tribes of Indians were formerly one, and all dwelt together on an island ... toward the east or sunrise ...' and that they arrived in the new land by floating in huge canoes 'for weeks.' The Iowa Indians also refer to an island point of origin in a legend which says: 'At first all men lived on an island where the day star is born.'

In South America, the pre-Inca Chimús, who developed an advanced civilization on the west coast of Peru, and an enormous ruined city, Chan Chan, whose ruins extend for more than eleven square miles, recorded that their ancestors arrived by sea in a great fleet of long canoes.

While not in accordance with the picturesque Indian legends of their point of origin, anthropologists do agree that the Indians did not originate on the American continent. One of the more cogent reasons given for the relatively recent appearance of man in the New World is the absence of fossil remains of large anthropoid apes or humanoid related species in America. Another is the fact that traces of man have not been found in a period generally argued as being between 10,000 to 30,000 years ago, while proto-man in Africa and Asia goes back one and a half to two million years.

Even the 10,000 year date was long considered excessive for for the residence of man in the Americas. When the fossil remains of a monstrous 'buffalo' (*bos americanus*), extinct for 10,000 years, was found in the '20s near Folsom, New Mexico, with a finely shaped grooved arrowhead among the bones, 'experts' proclaimed it an Indian arrowhead that had somehow been carried in among the bones by some sort of rodent.

132

Subsequently, when another arrowhead was found in one of the ribs of another extinct buffalo, opinion began to change, and eventually established Folsom man one of the continent's old inhabitants. Other traces of prehistoric man have turned up in different sections of the United States—one, for example, on the Atlantic coast of Florida, revealing fossils of saber tooth tigers and camels among the pottery and stone implements of man.

Although the horse is generally considered to have disappeared from the American continent before the advent of man, bones of primitive horses and men have been found *together* in several caves (Fells Cave, Cerro Sota and Pallo Aike) on the Strait of Magellan in 1938, and later dated to be more or less 9000 years old. This does not necessarily mean that the horse had been domesticated; the prehistoric Tierra del Fuegans may have been using the horse for food instead of transportation.

One comes across an even more surprising suggestion concerning the antiquity of man in South America. Near Pisco, Peru, in the general vicinity of the mysterious Nazca markings, among the ruins of two coastal cities constructed largely of porphery stone, discovered by Dr. Julio Tello, the Peruvian archaeologist, pottery has been found, decorated with representations of llamas. These llamas are shown as having five toes on each foot, instead of only two toes, or the cloven hoof, which llamas now have. But llamas *did* have five toes thousands of years ago.

Memories of extinct elephants and mastodons may account for the elephant motif in ancient Mexican art as well as the famous 'elephant mound' of Wisconsin. The same deduction can be made from pictures of the toxodon, a mammal we know existed in the area in remote ages, on pottery found in Tiahuanaco, Bolivia. Figures resembling dinosaurs have been found scratched on rock outcroppings and boulders in the Amazon Valley and small models of dinosaurs have been excavated in Central Mexico, and what look like dragons or enormous lizards are generally in evidence on temple friezes in various parts of Mexico and Central America.

Of course the Amazon pictographs may be simply representations of monsters or stylized lizard as in China, and in fact the Mayan dragons *do* resemble the Chinese dragons to an amazing degree. (The model dinosaurs, however, reputed to have been discovered in Acámbaro, Mexico, were in some disrepute even while they were being excavated, as it was found that local inhabitants were salting prospective digs with home-made clay dinosaurs of their own.) But, whatever the actual time element of man's residence in America, it is becoming increasingly evident that he has been here for a considerable time and certainly long enough to have been in contact with and influenced by other cultures, and not only those of Siberia via the Bering Strait.

Among the culturally more advanced nations of ancient America there was a curious and persistent tradition of repeated visits by white skinned, bearded gods, demigods, and teachers. In ancient Mexico this was the 'fair god' Quetzalcóatl, associated with the planet Venus and partial to flower offerings instead of the human sacrifices offered to the darker gods at that time. Quetzalcóatl is credited with having taught many of the arts of civilization to the predecessors of the Aztecs and to have come from a place in the eastern sea, variously called Tula, Tollán or Hue Hue (old, old) Tlapallan. Besides his pale skin coloring and beard Quetzalcóatl was also noteworthy in that he wore long garments embroidered with crosses.

A similar god, with the same background, was revered in the Maya lands as Kukulkán. Atlantologists find the Quetzalcóatl–Kukulkán legend an important keystone of what might be called the arch of the Atlantean theory, while others consider that he may have been Minoan, Phoenician, Carthaginian, Roman, or Viking, and the Irish, with unbridled Celtic enthusiasm, believe he may have been St. Brendan, who sailed with an expedition of monks from Tralee, Ireland, to the west in 484 A.D. and never returned, or that perhaps he was the mighty Irish warrior chief Cuchulain, because of the similarity of his name to Kukulkán.

The Mayas traditionally remember other fair-skinned

teachers coming from and returning to the 'island or land of the sea where the sun rises.' The Quiché-Maya nation of Guatemala called the teaching god Gucumatz. Itzamna, the Maya god of medicine, writing, and books, seems to be still another example of culture being important to ancient America. In Colombia, the Sun God of the Chibchas, Bochica, resembles Quetzalcóatl in his attributes of teacher and bringer of civilization. An unusual aspect of the Bochica legend, however, is that the god and his wife came to Colombia from the east riding camels. Samé, the semi-divine teacher whose memory was kept by the Indians of Brazil, and who taught them agriculture and magic, was also reputed to have come to Brazil from across the oceans where the sun rises. Like Quetzalcóatl and the other mysterious teachers he possessed an un-Indian white beard.

A somewhat different but equally intriguing legend was transcribed into Spanish by the Bishop of Chiapas in 1691 after the same bishop had caused to be burned the original Maya books from which he got his information. The account concerns a group of long-robed colonists coming to the Maya lands at a time calculated by the bishop and his assistant at about 1000 B.C. They were led by a demigod called Votan, sometimes referred to as a grandson of Quetzalcóatl, and he and his followers were said to have intermarried with the Mayas and founded the city of Palenque. An especially interesting feature of the Votan legend recounts that he went back several times to his own land across the ocean to bring back more followers.

These persistent legends may well have proven a crucial factor in the collapse of the Aztec Empire and later the Mayan cities under the Spanish onslaught for, by an incredible coincidence, Cortez and his army of conquistadors arrived on the 'name-year' *ce-acatl* (one reed), of the god Quetzalcóatl almost as if he had arrived for his own birthday exactly as the god had prophesied he would someday return, when he sailed off to Hue Hue Tlapallan. When the Aztecs saw the fair colouring of the Spaniards they were fairly sure they were the emissaries of Quetzalcóatl and that Cortez or perhaps the blond Captain Alvarado, whom they named Tonantiuh (Child of the Sun) was either the god himself or a close relative. At the beginning of the struggle the Aztecs, a basically warlike and combative nation, were greatly confused and divided inasmuch as they subconsciously felt that the war might be against the will of the gods, a phenomenon not necessarily restricted to that period of history.

The enormous Inca Empire, extending from Colombia to Chile and inland to Bolivia in South America, estimated by some authorities to contain 20,000,000 well-regimented and socialistically governed inhabitants fell for the same reason; their own god and teacher, Viracocha (Windy Sea), was said to have come from the great ocean and to have returned to a land to the west—a reversal of the Quetzalcóatl–Kukulkán legend. When the ancient Peruvians were suddenly confronted by the Spaniards, they could not escape the feeling that Pizarro and his men were somehow related to Viracocha. Their will to resist was further affected by a prophecy made by the twelfth Inca, Huayna Kapac, who prophesied while he was dying that, in the reign of the thirteenth Inca, 'White men would come from the Sun and conquer the Peruvians.'

The incidence of prophecy mixed with the traditions of godlike benefactors from the sea is one of the most unusual aspects of the conquest of native American Indian civilizations. The sister of the last Aztec Emperor, the Princess Papantzin, also correctly foretold the appearance of white gods from the sea on the coast of Mexico, a prophecy which so affected her brother, Montezuma, that when the Spaniards arrived he was incapable of action. Chilám Balám, a High Priest of the Mayas, also prophesied that at the end of the 13th Age white men would arrive again in Yucatán.

There was a further Aztec prophecy however, which implied that after the coming of the white men and the destruction of the old gods and their temples a day would come when the old gods and the old rule would once more be established in the valley of Mexico, a prophecy that is still kept alive among some of the unassimilated Indian tribes, however uncertain the date of fulfilment.

As they pursued their trail of conquest through ancient America the Spanish conquistadors found remnants of both light and dark skinned races. In a town named Atlán on the Atlantic coast of Panama they found light-skinned town dwellers whose women were the color, as they remembered it, of the women of Spain, but, in the enthusiasm of this discovery, all further anthropological comment, if it ever existed, has been lost.

Very dark, almost black, and also extremely war-like tribes were also encountered in the jungles of South America and, when the Spanish reached Peru they noted that the hereditary aristocracy of the Inca Empire was extremely fair skinned, sometimes with brown, red or blond hair while the selected and beautiful Virgins of the Sun were found by the conquering Spaniards to have the lightest skins of all.

The ancient Peruvians mummified their dead, like the Egyptians, and used some of the same general mummification techniques, such as removal of the viscera, embalming, and providing the mummy with possessions and objects of value for his or her trip to the next world. This thoughtful custom has naturally caused robbing and sacking of tombs in Egypt and Peru for generations. In the case of Peru it has led to a startling anthropological discovery—many of the ancient Peruvians had auburn or ash-blond hair, just as the early Spaniards saw them when they were alive.

Other bearded figures, of notably un-Indian features, sometimes in groups, can be seen carved in the Maya ruins at Chichén Itzá in Yucatán and at Tres Zapotes and La Venta near Vera Cruz, as well as numerous small clay and stone figures frequently being unearthed in Mexico and Central America which also bear distinctly un-Indian features, often resembling Semitic facial characteristics. In the vicinity of Vera Cruz where these statues, carvings, and plaques have been identified enormous carved basalt heads have also been found, whose features are distinctly Negroid. These huge heads, some weighing about 24 tons and standing more than six feet high, were excavated at Tres Zapotes where they had sunk almost out of sight into the jungle soil. These heads resemble similar heads with helmets found in La Venta, in the state of Tabasco, near the sea. Further inland, in ruins at Monte Albán, a frieze of dancers carved on building blocks shows both distinctive non-Indian types of racial features— Negroid and Semitic.

Reverse side of pre-Columbian mirror, found near Vera Cruz, Mexico. The head portrayed seems to be strikingly alien to Amerindian art, although somewhat suggestive of that of Egypt, Crete, or Phoenicia.

These carvings and smaller artifacts (including the wheeled toys or models) are generally attributed to the Olmec culture, the most ancient presently attributed to Mexico. In contemplating the juxtaposition of these various non-Indian races one is reminded of the mention in the Maya records—the *Popul Vuh*—of a former land 'where whites and blacks dwelt together in peace,' parenthetically, an unusual observation for a continent whose inhabitants were neither black nor white.

Constance Irwin, authoress of *Fair Gods and Stone Faces*, offers an imaginative explanation of the apparent racial anach-

138

ronisms in ancient Mexico. She suggests that the Semitic-looking people portrayed on friezes and small statues were Phoenician traders, a supposition supported by the type of clothes, shoes, and helmets they were wearing, or later, Carthaginian fugitives from the Roman destruction of Carthage and that the negroid dancers at Monte Albán as well as the colossal heads at La Venta and Tres Zapotes represented Africans who came with them, perhaps as slaves. This, however, would not explain why the colossal heads were made of Africans, whose presumed condition of slavery would not imply glorification on a level comparable to the Pharaonic statues of Egypt. And, finally, besides the racial mystery of the huge heads, one wonders whether the heads were part of enormous columns, like the supporting 'Atlantean' columns of the present archaeological site of Tula, Mexico, or whether they were parts of statues which have disappeared or which were never assembled.

The currents of the Atlantic Ocean would, it is true, make one-way travel to the Americas fairly easy on the southern route of the North Atlantic current, leaving the Western European shores with the Canaries current and, with the help of prevailing winds, catching the northern equatorial current and sailing to the northeast coast of South America or, through the Antilles into the Caribbean Sea where landings could be made in Venezuela, Colombia, and the coast of Central America up to Yucatán and around the Yucatán Peninsula into Vera Cruz. This would explain numerous mysteries such as the cache of Roman coins found in Venezuela, the hundreds of Phoenician inscriptions in Brazil and the riddles of La Venta and Tres Zapotes. It would also explain the reputed, though not officially accepted, vestiges of Mediterranean or other unidentified cultures on the coast of the United States from Florida to Maine which would be of easy access to voyagers from the south because of the Gulf Stream and winds.

Conversely, the Gulf Stream flowing north and the North Atlantic Current might logically take seafaring American Indians to Europe, as apparently happened in the first century A.D. when a long canoe with copper-skinned occupants from parts unknown washed ashore in Northern Europe from the North Sea, were taken into custody and presented as slaves to the Roman Proconsul Publius Metellus Cellar. There is even a Roman bust made of one of these Atlantic travelers whose features, in the representational style of Roman art, definitely show the characteristics of an American Indian. Even Christopher Columbus noted two corpses washed ashore in Galway, Ireland, in a long boat, who looked 'Chinese,' but who were most probably Indians or Eskimos, thus unknowingly besting Columbus on the very eve of his great achievement.

The Viking settlers in Greenland and early visitors to America could also have used favorable currents—the east and west Greenland currents going west and the Labrador current going down the coast of Newfoundland from where they could easily penetrate the Gulf of St. Lawrence to Nova Scotia, the Island of Newfoundland, and other points south along the coast. Despite the fact that such voyages across the Atlantic, especially through the north and from West Africa to Brazil are of considerably shorter duration than the longer voyages apparently taken by the South Sea Islanders in smaller craft, there has been a long reticence on the American continent to accept as factual any report of transatlantic voyages before Columbus. Charles Michael Bowen, a researcher of early voyages to America, has coined a phrase for this tendency which he calls 'the NEBC principle,' prepresenting 'No-Europeans-Before-Columbus.' In his book *They All Discovered America* he traces in detail the fairly well-documented probable pre-Columbian voyages of Cortereal of Portugal (1477); the Scot, Prince Henry Sinclair and the Zeno brothers of Venice (1395); the Norse Paul Knutson (1355); Prince Madoc of Wales (1171); Bishop Eric Gnupsson, dispatched by the Vatican (1121); Thorfinn Karlseffni, an Icelander (1010); the Vikings Leif (1003) and Thorvald Ericsson (1007) and other transatlantic travelers, less documented and still farther away in the mist of time. However, until the present there has been little possibility of establishing the credibility of pre-Columbian voyages and even less the probability of transatlantic or inter-Atlantic contact in ancient times.

The American tribes and nations recorded these visits from the sea as legends, while the visitors often returned home and wrote about where they had been, with some understandable exaggeration. The Northmen kept chronicles of Greenland (which hardly seems green now although it was warmer then and former villages, built of stone, are still under the ice), Vinland, the land of grapes, probably New England, while the land where St. Brendan discovered a previously emigrated colony of Irish monks already living there, sounds like Bermuda, the Bahamas, the Greater Antilles or even the east coast of Florida.

Several New World locations, in addition to such names as the West Indies, Indians, etc., owe their names to the fact that Europeans gave them names of legendary lands reported to be in the vicinity of those they had just found. They are the Antilles, the English version of Antilla, which may be related to Atlantis itself, and the word Brazil or Hy Brazil, a mysterious western land of Irish legend. Strangely enough, the enigmatic phrase Hy Brazil (*I BRZL*) means 'isle of iron' in the ancient semitic languages, with B-R-Z-L still meaning iron in modern Hebrew. The 'Isle of Iron' repeated as a name of a western land by the Irish who did not know the meaning of the phrase seems to be an apt designation for iron-rich Brazil, the land which, when discovered, was given the name of the mysterious 'island of iron.'

Chinese expeditions may have visited North America from the west. The Hai King (circa 2250 B.C.) describes a crossing of the 'Great East Ocean' and a long southward trip from their landing place, including an inland excursion to a 'great luminous rock wall valley'—presumed to be the Grand Canyon. Another more southern trans-Pacific voyage in a large ocean-going junk was recorded by a Chinese Buddhist priest, Hwui Shin, in the fifth century A.D., during the period of Chinese history referred to as the Six Dynasties. He called the lands he visited across the sea Fusang, Chinese for 'aloe-tree,' and his contemporaneous descriptions of them seem to describe Mexico (which has aloe trees) and Central America. Voyages

141

from the Orient such as that of Hwui Shin or earlier ones may account for the marked 'dragon' influence in ancient Mexican art as well as representations of the lotus, the swastika (which the Chinese called 'Heart of Buddha' more than 2000 years before Hitler heard of it), and other Oriental motifs. The Orientals who brought the mythical dragon motif and perhaps travelers from the ancient Mediterranean as well, may even have seen the American 'buffalo' which must have seemed as extraordinary to them as a real dragon. A comment written in old Turkish script on the American side of the Piri Reis map speaks of 'monsters seven spans long. Between their eyes is a distance of one span. But they are harmless souls . . .'

None of the vestiges or messages that may have been left on the American continents by historical travelers or colonists before Columbus has been accepted. Most of the examples have been labeled hoaxes. The famous Kensington Stone unearthed in 1898 by a Minnesota farmer is an outstanding example. Purporting to be a record of Goths or Swedes and Norwegians journey from 'Vinland West,' it detailed an attack on their camp and an appeal for help. The fact that the stone was found by a descendant of Vikings in a Scandinavian community is perhaps not the most insignificant reason, after generations of argument, for its rejection by non-Scandinavians. Less easy to explain away from the point of national or ethnic pride is the case of the numerous, literally thousands of Phoenician or Carthaginian inscriptions in Brazil, of which one, a stone tablet found in the state of Paraíba in 1872 and acrimoniously debated ever since, reads in part . . . 'We are . . . from Sidon . . . Commerce has cast us on this distant shore, a land of mountains . . .' and giving as ten the original number of ships that had sailed from a Phoenician port on the Gulf of Aqaba, quite near the present Israeli port of Elath. Although it was long considered a forgery, it seems illogical that Brazilians should so consistently forge Phoenician inscriptions and then bury them in out-of-the-way places. An authority on ancient Semitic languages, Professor Cyrus Gordon, in 1968 stated that, in his opinion, a putative forger could not have known of or used certain aspects of Phoenician writing style that were not yet known to philologists back in 1872.

Even more difficult to counterfeit would be the carved representation of a ship resembling an ancient Phoenician or Minoan vessel incised on a rock in Lake Assawompset, Massachusetts. The difficulty in this case would reside in the fact that the enormous carved boulder is underwater and was only temporarily revealed when the waterline was lowered during the drought of 1957. It is to be noted that if the waterline of the sea were considerably lower at some time in the remote past, the level of inshore waters would also tend to be lower, thereby not only explaining this presently underwater carving of an ancient ship but also would be one explanation of underwater buildings in lakes in certain areas of New England and also in Haiti. Vestiges of incursions of prehistoric cultures into North America, therefore, would generally tend to be found underwater on the continental shelf and under the waters of the coastal bays, inlets, and sounds.

On land, however, there have been several discoveries made in widely separated points indicating settlements in the eastern United States by people belonging to a Mediterranean or possibly Atlantic culture. Such remnants are so unexpected that they are frequently not recognized and undergo all kinds of modifications, disparagement, and destruction prior to detailed study. A good example is the megalithic buildings of Mystery Hill, North Salem, New Hampshire, where 25 miles from the present Atlantic coastline, twenty-two ruined stone structures stand on top of a 200-foot hill. These structures, originally called Pattee's Caves, as Jonathan Pattee was the first settler known to occupy the hill, were simply incorporated by him into his cellar and storage system without questioning their antiquity or how they got there. Subsequently the stone buildings suffered a common archaeological fate— they were used as a stone quarry, in this case to build the sewers of Lawrence, Massachusetts.

What remained of the ruins was finally acquired by the New England Antiquities Research Association which, under the direction of Robert Stone, is operating a continuous program of research to establish the identity and date of the buildings now tentatively dated, through Carbon-14 dating of surface charcoal over the ruins, from 1225 to 865 B.C.

Theories concerning the builders of these megalithic non-mortared passageways, tunnels, rock rooms, menhirs, dolmans, and what appears to be a sacrificial stone, attribute them to Phoenicians, Carthaginians, Minoans, Irish monks, and even Indians or, in the words of one critic, endeavoring to explain the identity of those who had conceived the apparently haphazard plan of the ruins; 'Indians—drunk.' Robert Stone, whose closeness to the ruins has not fostered insularism, but on the contrary, has impelled him to search for an explanation through comparison with archaeological sites throughout the world, is of the opinion that they are megalithic structures similar to those found on the Iberian Peninsula, especially in Portugal, and resembling somewhat prehistoric buildings in Malta, Sardinia, and other Mediterranean islands.

No identifiable writing has yet been translated from Mystery Hill although letters or symbols have been found which seem to resemble Phoenician or a similar alphabet. Other apparently Phoenician letters were found in Mechanicsburg, Pennsylvania, starting in 1948, when about one thousand grooved stones were found, marked not with inscriptions but with single Phoenician letters. Charles M. Boland, who studied the matter with Dr. William Strong of Mechanicsburg, suggests that these strange grooved stones were especially cut to fit together according to alphabetical coding.

Sometimes what had been previously thought to be fairly recent Indian petroglyphs or writing have been found to represent understandable words in Phoenician or Minoan or a similar language. A fascinating instance is a stone found in 1885 near Morganton in Loudon County, Tennessee, thought to be an inscription in Cherokee, as the Cherokee nation in Georgia had developed their own alphabet before their exile to the west. However, although the letters do resemble some signs of the Cherokee script, when the stone is turned upside down they spell, in the opinion of Dr. Cyrus Gordon of Brandeis University, an authority on ancient civilizations and languages, the inscription 'For Jehu' in Canaanite, an illustrative example of scholars having looked at an inscription upside down for eighty-five years.

More recently, in 1968, Manfred Metcalf, a civilian employee of Fort Benning, Georgia, while choosing stones for a barbecue pit, found one with an incription, also eventually verified by Dr. Gordon and Dr. Joseph Mahan of the Columbus Museum of Art as being Minoan script, showing numbers and also the Minoan symbol of the double axe.

There are other frequent reports of finds and sites, as yet uncatalogued, owing their survival to the population shift from the New England and mid-Atlantic countryside to the cities, to the West, and also to the Eastern metropolitan centres. Whole sections of farmlands have gone back to second growth in some areas and with this return to comparative wilderness, American artifacts on a time scale comparable to the Bronze or perhaps the Stone Age have been forgotten or remain undiscovered or unrecognized. It is in these areas, reverted to scrub forest and underbrush, and on the bottom of lakes, rivers, and coastal waters above the old shore line that further remnants of megalithic or pre-Indian culture may be found in North America.

Several stone step-pyramids, shunned by the occasional Seminole Indians who claim to have seen them, have been reported to stand in the Big Cypress Swamps of the Everglades, southwest of Okeechobee; north of the toll road between Fort Lauderdale and Naples, Florida, in the road section called 'Alligator Alley.' Such mounds or pyramids may have been built by pre-Indians or by the Caloosa Indians who have left pyramid-shaped mounds faced with shells as well as sophisticated pottery and artifacts on the Florida coast and cays, and who themselves may have been the remnants of an older culture. As it becomes evident that American archaeology is much older than was previously considered former finds are being re-examined and reassessed. In West Virginia, in a mysterious mountain cave above the Kanawha Valley, near Chelyan, in the vicinity of a long stone wall running along the top of Mount Carbon a large wooden statue was discovered in 1896, representing a woman carrying a buffalo calf. The local

Cherokee and Shawnee Indians were not in the habit of carving large wooden statues and, when questioned about who built the wall, replied in the manner of South American Indians asked similar questions, that a white race had once lived in the valley before them. This 'Buffalo Madonna' subsequently gave rise to theories of pre-Indians having domesticated the buffalo for food, leather, or transportation of people or materials. The Buffalo Madonna is now on exhibition in Montreal, Canada, and is considered to be an unusual piece of historic art, part of the Mound Builder culture, the Adena in particular, which goes back to about 1500 B.C.

The civilization of the Mound Builders represents another archaeological discovery no less mysterious since it is closer at hand, although much of the evidence is fast vanishing through the depredations of time and bulldozers.

The first settlers of the central and southern United States found thousands of mounds or truncated pyramids throughout the Mississippi and Ohio Valleys and almost all of the waterways of the midwest and the Gulf region. Some were huge, the Cahokia Mound in Illinois covered 16 acres and was as high as a 10-storey building, some were small and apparently tombs, some were in the shape of animals—the Serpent Mound near Louden, Ohio, is the largest representation of a snake in the world with open jaws 60 feet long, and some were apparently high platforms for vanished temples. Others appear to have been individual platforms for groups of buildings or whole cities protected by earthwork walls. Dr. James Ford of the American Museum of Natural History, referring to the dimensions of the earthworks of a mound 'city' at Poverty Point, Louisiana, with datings from 1300 to 200 B.C., calculates it as being 'over 35 times the cubage of the Great Pyramid.'

The early settlers at first largely ignored the mounds, except as handy refuges from floods, under the stress of more pressing circumstances connected with survival. When they got around to asking the Indians about the mounds the answer was usually that they had been built long ago by ancient peoples whose identity was unknown even to the

Indians. The settlers destroyed or obliterated many mounds in clearing their lands or in building over or around the mounds. Later they dug into them looking for treasure. One mound complex owes its preservation to the fact that it is presently incorporated into a golf course in Newark, Ohio.

During the nineteenth century, interest in the Mound Builders reached a crescendo in a young United States, psychologically desirous of having its own traditions of extreme antiquity. Robert Silverberg in his entertaining study *The Mound Builders of Ancient America* has traced some of the overenthusiasm on the part of the researchers of that era who, noting the unusual sculptures, animal effigies, copper artifacts, helmets, weapons, and semiprecious jewels—jadite and pearls—found in the mounds, saw in the Mound Builders such varied peoples as Atlanteans, Welsh, or even the Ten Lost Tribes of Israel. They attributed to these mysterious pre-Indians enormous cities and the domestication of the buffalo *and* the mastodon and supposed that both of these unlikely helpers contributed to the construction of the enormous mounds and earthworks.

Succeeding generations have taken a more dubious look at the Mound Builders and some informed opinion shares Silverberg's view that the mounds were made by the more advanced ancestors of Indian tribes who later forgot about them or retrogressed culturally past the organization point necessary for continued construction. A certain skepticism has arisen as well concerning finds within the thousands of mounds which have been opened and despoiled through the last 160 years. In one ancient Wisconsin mound an interesting silver bracelet was found with letters on it which, upon examination, spelled 'Montreal,' while a metal plate found in an Illinois mound had an inscription resembling Chinese characters. It turned out to *be* Chinese, albeit an unlikely artifact, being a brand name for tea. However, the fact that some Indians still used the mounds for burial in recent times, or that interested persons occasionally attempt to bend history to America's prehistory does not change the importance of these ancient mounds.

It now seems evident that the pyramid-like mounds of the southern Mississippi and Gulf region were influenced by the cultures of Mexico while the northern mounds may have been subject to other, perhaps older, influences. If the mounds in the United States were built by culturally advanced Indian tribes who subsequently forgot about them it would seem to conform with the retrograde tendency of American and numerous other ancient cultures, wherein as one goes farther back in time one finds more advanced cultural patterns in the preceding eras than in the succeeding centuries. This is true in Mexico, where the Aztecs had not improved on the civilization of their predecessors, the Toltecs or the Olmecs and in fact, although retaining great scientific knowledge, art, and literature, also practiced human sacrifice and cannibalism; in the Maya lands, where civilization had run down even before the Spanish conquest; and in the Inca Empire of South America whose buildings, remarkable as they were, were not comparable to those built before them, and who reputedly remembered the loss of the art of writing.

This is also patently true in the case of the islands of the Pacific, where island centers of civilization once capable of erecting stone cities and enormous statues had relapsed into barbarism and cannibalism. Evidence of how a civilization can run down and literally disappear once its impetus is interrupted or lost can be observed in some of the great cities of Southeast Asia abandoned within recorded times. These include the lost Temple cities of Ankor Wat and Ankor Thom in Cambodia, of which only the carved stone temples and palaces remain—the wooden houses of the large metropolitan population having deteriorated and completely disappeared in a thousand years; and the enormous jungle cities of Ceylon, long known only by tradition, Anuradhapura and Polannaruwa, the former stretching 16 miles from gate to gate and containing an estimated population of more than a million people.

More lost cities in the jungles of Central America may throw more light on American and world prehistory. They are usually first located from the air, when groups of frequent and oddly symmetrical tree-covered hills rise suddenly from the jungle. Such formations have often proven to be temple and palace complexes of Maya cities.

There are persistent and intriguing legends, periodically revived, concerning still undiscovered lost cities in the jungles of Brazil or the Amazon in which the descendants of Stone Age builders are reputed still to be living. These cities, especially one called Manoa, have been reported since the Spanish and Portugese first arrived in the area, looking for gold, and the description given to Francisco López by Indians at the time of the conquest of Peru contained elements to appeal to any treasure hunter ... 'Ma-Noa is on an island in a great salt lake. Its walls and roof are made of gold and reflected in a gold tiled lake. All the serving dishes for the palace ... are made of pure gold and silver, and even the most insignificant things are made of silver and copper ... In the middle of the island stands a temple dedicated to the Sun. Around the building there are statues of gold which represent giants. There are also trees made of gold and silver on the island ... and the statue of a prince covered entirely with gold dust.'

Frequent reports of such a treasure laden city, sometimes inhabited by white Indians and surrounded by dangerous wild tribes or sometimes deserted, have been reported for hundreds of years concerning the Amazon region and north to the Guyanas and Venezuela and have indirectly contributed considerably to the exploration of the area. Even Sir Walter Raleigh unsuccessfully tried to find it in 1595. Fired by the reports of a certain Raposa, who claimed to have visited the city in 1743, in 1764 a Brazilian expedition of four hundred men set out for Manoa under Bodavilla, of whom only twenty-five unsuccessful seekers returned. On another occasion an entire Brazilian army of 1400 men vanished into the jungle. The search for the golden city or cities of Manoa has claimed distinguished victims in our own day, Colonel Fawcett in 1925 and more recently the French explorer, R. Manfrais, in 1950.

Bearing in mind that large 'lost cities' have actually been found in the American jungles, from the famous mountaintop 'lost city' of Machu Picchu in Peru, discovered in the early part of the twentieth century, to the jungle-hidden 3500-year-old Mayan metropolis of Dzibilchaltún, not located until about twenty years ago, although it is located only a few miles away from Mérida in Yucatán, it is certainly possible that one or more large stone cities have so far escaped discovery in Brazil or on the southern borders of Venezuela and the Guyanas, where recent frequent sightings of such cities have been claimed by pilots who have, however, failed to find them on subsequent flights, a not unreasonable failure given the size of the area.

What is more doubtful, although again not impossible, is that there should be living survivors of ancient cultures who now dwell in secret South American cities surrounded by almost impassable territories, peopled by tribes distinguished by a lack of enthusiasm for strangers and by an efficient use of poison darts. As to the recurring tales of gold told to so many explorers by the Indians, this may be traceable to the understandable desire of the Indians, once they ascertained what the seekers were after, to send them on a quest out of the immediate area, on to the next river, the next valley, the next range of mountains, anywhere but the place where they were.

But the words of Fawcett, his final ones in effect, since he never returned from his last expedition, hold a sort of fascination, not only for seekers of gold but also for those who seek to explore the past and to illumine its dark and hidden places. He said:

One thing is certain: the answer to the riddle of South America—and perhaps of the entire prehistoric world—may be found when the site of those ancient cities is fixed and made accessible to scientific exploration. This much I know: the cities exist ... I myself have seen a part of them —and that is the reason why I feel compelled to go back ... The remains appear to be the outposts of greater cities which ... I am convinced can be discovered if a properly organized search can be carried out. Unfortunately, I am not successful in persuading scientists even to accept the

150

bare supposition that Brazil contains the traces of an ancient civilization. I have travelled in many regions ... The Indians have told me again and again about the buildings, the characteristics of the people, and all the strange things in the land beyond ...

Besides lost cities in the jungle, on almost inaccessible mountains, or submerged as ruins on the continental shelf, other important finds relative to early American archaeology or vestiges of visitors to ancient America from other places, may have already been found within the cave systems of Yucatán. The Loltún Cave complex in the Púuc Hills of Central Yucatán is an outstanding example. In the words of Dr. Manson Valentine, an archaeologist and zoologist who has made important discoveries there, it is

Perhaps the most important underground complex, archaeologically, in America. Ancient and widely disseminated legends refer to it. The name, Loltún, means, 'Flower in Stone' so-called, we believe, because of its unique arrangement of spacious corridors and chambers leading off, like the petals of a gigantic flower, from the vast entrance vestibule. The stone flower, recalling the lotus, is an archaic and much venerated, universal symbol, found on many sacred buildings and ornamenting the foreheads of gods throughout the ancient world, including the Mayan. It is also closely associated with that most meaningful and ubiquitous of all symbols, the circle-cross, with which Loltún might be compared if we take into account the various passageways connecting, as it were, the spokes of the wheel. Here, in this fabulous cavern, known to man and utilized by him continuously from a remote time beyond the possibility of accurate measurement, is abundant proof that the many weird carvings, modified formations and glyphs are not the work of the Maya but of some older race or races ...

Among Dr. Valentine's more unusual finds were colossal

states, apparently carved at an extremely early date from rock pillars, stalactites or stalagmites within the caves. Evidences of water marks within the caves and on these statues indicate that the caves, now several hundred feet above sea level, had been under water *after* the strange stone figures were carved. The theory that the whole limestone section of the area had been under the sea was further verified when divers, exploring the nearby sacred wells or *cenotes*, brought up oceanic marine growth from the sacred pools.

Although generations of the Maya apparently occupied the Loltún Cave complex, which is still largely unexplored, the older statues, made before the caves were flooded, seem to have been carved by people from a completely different culture, reminiscent sometimes of the ancient Middle East. In the words of Dr. Valentine:

One such figure, a nine-foot sinister giant with a full beard, appears to be winged and his body is vertically and horizontally perforated with holes running clear through him, most likely to support torches or other ceremonial accessories ... The strangest and most important thing about Loltún, however, is the fact that there are countless stone carvings representing faces of men, animals, gods, etc. Many of these, including the numerous petroglyphs, are in no way similar to Mayan carvings; and the faces are usually the faces of men with full beards ...'

As usual in the case of very ancient remains of cultures in the Americas, the indigenous races living at or near the site have only vague legends concerning them. Dr. Valentine observed:

The present-day Maya say that they [as a race] had nothing whatsoever to do with such carvings in Loltún and nearby caves. They say these things were placed there by the 'first inhabitants' of Yucatán, the small, hunch-backed men they call 'Púus.' These men were supposed to have been completely destroyed by a catastrophe that swept the

Yucatán in remote times, destroying everything on the surface and leaving only the carvings in the caves as reminders that they had passed that way. The Maya say that later their ancestors, the first Maya, entered and found these strange remnants of the 'Púus.'

It would be natural for subsequent peoples to attribute unusual physical characteristics to their predecessors, as has frequently happened in other parts of the earth, with legends of small peoples, usually living in caves, or the frequent legends of ancient giants. The dwarfs or trolls would seem to be attributed their shape for easy access into and within caverns, while the giants, as in the case of the Andean lands, Ireland, the Mediterranean, North Africa and the Pacific islands are given their increased stature to explain the construction of otherwise unexplainable buildings.

Members of a race distinct from the native inhabitants of coasts and islands who first saw them would, of course, look strange and exotic to the indigenes, and would so be represented in pictorial artifacts made of them, either at the time of their visits or copied from time to time from surviving models of statues, bas reliefs, or pictures. The features of such representations would tend to conserve their facial and physical points of difference from the local populations, immortalizing in this way the Mediterranean and African features of ancient American artifacts and the strange other-worldly look of the Easter Island monoliths as well as the strangely dressed figures in the Tassili rock drawings in North African caves and caves in the Kalahari Desert of South Africa, and the unidentified 'people of the sea' pictured on the ancient Egyptian wall paintings of Medinet Habu. Even the most ancient legends of Sumeria, at a place that we usually suppose to have seen the birth of civilization, told that civilization was brought to Sumeria from the sea.

A unifying theme common to such legends that have come down to us concerning visits to tribes and nations by 'gods from the sea' is that they are usually reputed to have come in peace, bringing civilization with them, a notable exception

153

being Plato's account of a war-like Atlantean army conveniently stopped by the determination of the people of Plato's own city, Athens.

At the risk of attributing contemporary motives to peoples so ancient that we have no idea of their aims or designs, one might suggest that perhaps these 'gods from the sea' or sea peoples came to outlying places in the then undeveloped sections of the world in order to establish industries—teaching the native populations how to make certain things, jewelry, pottery, cloth, stone carvings, so that they could pick up ship-

Prehistoric cave painting from Kalahari Desert, South Africa. Costume of figure portrayed is unusual for the time and place, apparently showing gloves, boots, and other unidentifiable accouterments.

ments of these artifacts to trade in the civilized parts of the world, many of which may now be lying under water or even under ice. Then, when they failed to return (perhaps for reasons of catastrophic occurrences in their own lands), the populations of these various outposts went on waiting for the 'gods from the sea' to come again, and kept on repeating the manufacture of the things they had been trained to make. But, as time went on and one generation learned the crafts from the other, their craftsmanship grew less precise, and finally even the memory of why they were doing these things, or who made the originals they had copied, was lost.

There is an eerie parallel in our own time period. The New Guinea natives, during World War II, were delighted that the 'white gods' in flying machines came to their country, bringing all sorts of amazing inventions and treasures, which they prodigiously distributed to the bemused and enchanted natives and even gave them magic medicines to cure some of their diseases. To this day, in remote villages, they wait for the white gods their fathers knew during the great years from 1942 to 1945, and they *and* their descendants continue to make pitiful effigies of airfields, planes, jeeps, and windsocks from earth, sticks, stones, and cloth, with the hope that the miraculous visits of the gods from the sky will someday come again.

CHAPTER NINE

THE TIME CURTAIN AND THE LOST AGES
OF MAN

If an advanced culture existed prior to our present concepts of ancient civilization having started in the Middle East, we must ask ourselves not only about possible traces of such civilization but also whether the time era was of sufficient duration to foster the growth of civilization in certain tracts of the earth's surface, some of which may have been submerged in the ensuing centuries.

The time curtain has been pushed back within recent years at a rate bordering on the vertiginous. Dr. Louis Leaky's finds in Africa, although not universally accepted as final, indicate that a form of man existed in Olduvai Gorge in Tanzania as long ago as 1,500,000 to 2,000,000 years. At this point Carbon-14 can no longer be used as a measure of age (it is more or less effective only up to 50,000 years) and some other system such as potassium argon dating must be applied to the deposits in which human remains and artifacts are found. A wall or windbreak, possibly built by human hands, has been identified as belonging to this incredibly early period. A crude wall, of course, is not necessarily a mark of either culture or civilization, since animals and insects build constructions, as in the well-known cases of beavers, birds, gophers, and ants and the somewhat lesser known case of the undersea dock and coral constructions of octopi. In addition, some of the great apes such as baboons have been known to use sticks and stones for war-like attacks on other baboon groups. Therefore the remains of ascendant man should perhaps be dated from the use of intelligent language, which we cannot yet estimate, or from the use of artificially modified stone tools, which as far as we know no animal has yet accomplished, pictures, the use of fire, and finally the domestication of animals and the cultivation of crops. It is fairly well established that chopping tools were used in the Vallonet caves of France about 1,000,000 years ago, as well as chipped stone axes in the Olduvai Gorge at a corresponding period, found clustered together with bones as if they were put their in a special câche, almost like a prehistoric toolshed.

Lights went on in the world, in the form of the ability to make fire, from 700,000 to 500,000 years ago. This important step of civilization, referred to in ancient legend immortalizing Prometheus, who stole the fire of the gods, may be an over-simplified but useful measuring stick of a time when man first began to be clearly defined from his anthropoid cousins. Evidences of man-made fires of extreme age have been found in Asia, Africa, and Europe; in China, specifically in Chou-Kou-Tien, near Peking, human skulls have been found in close promixity to datable ash remains.

The present age we live in, the Holocene, goes back 11,000 years, while the Pleistocene age, which preceded this, and was the age in which the glaciations occurred, is variously calculated as going back 500,000 to 2,000,000 years. Any consideration of the extreme antiquity of civilized man will therefore border on the end of the Pleistocene, a theory as yet unaccepted by many prehistorians, but increasingly more tenable as new information comes to light.

The general public impression of prehistoric man, fostered by the movies and TV, is that of a brutish ape-like creature, living in caves, clubbing his enemies, and gnawing on bones. Anthropological investigation of prehistory presents a somewhat different picture, representing prehistoric man as living in primitive groups or tribes and possessing tools and other artifacts. He is generally classified by the names of periods named after the towns or regions where certain typical tool-making techniques applied to stone or bone were first found, the culture level between Paleolithic, Mesolithic, and the more recent Neolithic culture being determined by whether the stone implements were merely chipped, as in the Paleolithic period, or polished and grooved as in the more advanced

157

Mesolithic and Neolithic ages starting, as far as presently determined, about 30,000 years ago.

As is natural in the study of a period so far removed in time, revisions of opinion about the import of prehistoric remains have been frequent. Up to the beginning of modern times, for example, the many prehistoric stone axes found in Europe were explained by the clergy, the then scientific authorities of the period, as being weapons thrown from heaven in the battles between God and Satan.

Even in modern times certain theories have been revised, such as theories about why so many crushed skulls of enormous cave bears were found in prehistoric caves—at first thought to be the results of sacrifice or related to food or the hunt. It is now considered that prehistoric cave dwellers, in disputing ownership of caves with their towering adversaries, the cave bears, were able to conceive long-range planning and would wait until the bears were in hibernation in order to drop rocks on their heads while they were sleeping.

Other anomalies are noticeable as we study the era of caves to which we may concede undue importance as living quarters simply because it is only in the depths of caves that certain relics of prehistoric culture have been preserved. Neanderthal man seems to have occupied Europe and to have been typical of man in other parts of the world for a protracted period, for perhaps 150,000 years. Prehistorians have recently been able to reconstruct his appearance—thick body, squat, with receding forehead, and very powerful.

About 30,000 to 34,000 years ago a new race, the Crô-Magnon, appeared in Europe, contemporaneous with but not descended from Neanderthal man and apparently caused the disappearance of the Neanderthal race in what may have been a war of extermination. The original Crô-Magnon man, in the opinion of most anthropologists, had a brain capacity superior to modern man and, by his development of weapons, food, statuettes, and paintings such as still exist in many caves in France and Spain, shows evidence of an incredible culture difference between himself and the Neanderthal man he apparently dispossessed. Crô-Magnon man was tall, straight, well formed and had a highly developed brain. Dr. Jerome Bruner, an authority on the development of human cognition, when recently asked the improbable question of how a Crô-Magnon youth would perform at a university, in this case Harvard, gave the opinion: 'He would not be conspicuously in bad shape.'

There is no evidence to suppose that the Crô-Magnon peoples grew out of the Neanderthal culture complex for, at all ages of human history, undeveloped and advanced tribes and nations have existed contemporaneously—usually, as has been true from Neanderthal times to the present, to the detriment of the more primitive whenever there was a direct confrontation.

It is within this 30,000 to 35,000 year time range therefore, with the sudden appearance of Crô-Magnon man (first appearing, it may be noted, on the Bay of Biscay on the Atlantic coast of France and Spain) that certain concrete indications of former advanced civilizations, prior to the generally accepted first civilizations of Egypt and Sumeria, may be recognized.

A peculiar feature of the appearance of Crô-Magnon man on the continent of Europe and North Africa is that different waves of culture seem to succeed each other, each one appearing suddenly. A look at a map of Europe with areas of prehistoric artifact and cave painting sites indicated by shading tends to convey the impression that the bringers of the new culture patterns came from the sea to the western shores of Europe. Such a theory, perhaps not so far-fetched when we consider the high incidence of boat drawings in Neolithic art, normally causes satisfied conviction on the part of those who hold for a pre-glacial Atlantean continent for, as Lewis Spence has pointed out, the appearance of new prehistoric cultures in Europe, such as the Aurignacian, Magdalenian, and Azilian (circa 32,000, 16,000, and 12,000 before the present era) roughly correspond to periodic sinkings of ocean lands projected either during retreat of the glaciers or even during the climatic or seismic disturbances connected with the last two glaciations. Also, if refugees from other parts of the earth arrived in Europe they would conserve only an imperfect part of their civilization, but would still be cultural light years ahead of their Neanderthal predecessors.

Oddly enough, bearing in mind the paucity of relics and artifacts at our disposal, something of this sort seems to have happened, not only with the arrival of the Crô-Magnon peoples but in a curious historic interval after they were already established in Europe. This concerns the appearance of the Solutrean culture, named after the town of Solutré, France, roughly coming between the longer periods—the Aurignacian and the Magdalenian—about 22,000 to 20,000 years ago. Some of the fanciful and delicate stone carvings, some of semiprecious stones, of these mysterious people serve no utilitarian purpose of which we presently can conceive. Unaccountably, at an age in the history of man where we usually consider that his efforts were directed almost entirely to keeping warm, catching food and endeavoring to keep from being caught himself, this unusual people made delicate, thin, and convoluted designs, using semiprecious stones in addition to the normal flints, almost as if they were trying to combine an art that was natural to them with a survival technique that had become necessary. Some of their knives and arrowheads are so fine that they could not have effectively served as weapons of warfare or the hunt and can therefore only be considered as ceremonial adjuncts or even adornment. Their cave paintings were strangely developed and sophisticated. Solutrian bone sewing needles, with small eyes, suggest that they were used to make carefully fitted and finely sewn leather or skin clothing; a concept widely at variance with the mental picture of an animal-like cave man clad in a bear skin thrown over his shoulders.

Prehistoric drawings found at Lussac, France, now under study at the Musée de l'Homme in Paris, depict people of Magdalenian times in well fitting and strangely modern looking clothes, casually drawn in an amazing mixture of styles—impressionistic, representational, and abstract. Some of the European and African cave paintings from the Aurignacian and Magdalenian eras are so modern, decorative, and sophisticated in technique that they have been thought to be modern

160

fakes, until long study by such authorities on prehistoric cave paintings as the late Abbé Breuil has proved them to be genuine. The opinion of the prehistorian Robert Silverberg is shared by many others who have seen these paintings: '... until as recently as 1400 the best painters of Europe had

Cave sketch from Lussac, France, of the Magdalenian Epoch, from 12,000 to 15,000 years old. Although this is one of the earliest naturalistic sketches of a human being the line technique is curiously modern and indicates garments not previously associated with people of such an early era. Curved needles made of bone in the Solurean era, however, suggest the capability of making fitted garments at a surprisingly early time period.

not understood how to impart such lifelike characteristics to their work ...'

It is not known exactly how or why these paintings were made—how, in the sense of the longevity of the pigments or how they were so exactly painted in dark caves. What form of illumination did they have? Apparently they did not use torches, since there are no signs of smoke blackening on the roof of the cave. The why is also open to question—as to whether the wild bulls, lions, mammoths, rhinoceroses, bears, gazelles, horses and other animals were ritual, for success in the hunt or simply illustrative. But the biggest why is why they were painted in caves so difficult of access, some of which, during the intervening thousands of years, have sunk and are now under the level of the ground.

The theory has been advanced that men of the Magdalenian era possessed dwellings and even towns outside of the caves where we now find their remains, but such constructions, unless made of stone (and prehistoric stone structures are most difficult to date) or preserved under water or in mud, would have vanished long ago. Moreover it is not inconceivable that Stone Age peoples could use cement, as testified by the unbelievably intricate use of cement by the Mayas of Central America and the invention of a fireproof cement by the Chibcha Indians of Colombia, both of which cultures being catalogued in the Stone Age. But over many centuries and type of structure—brick, plaster, stucco, or cement would deteriorate much faster in forests or areas subject to extreme climate changes than in a dry climate such as in Egypt and adjoining lands, which is precisely where we have found what is considered to be man's oldest towns and cities, a walled city at Jericho and ruins at the Wadi el Natuf going back 10,000 years. It is also possible that the archaic stone structures of the western coasts of Europe, the Mediterranean, and the Americas are older than previously considered and the possibility that they may have been repaired or partially rebuilt by successive generations would tend to make them appear more recent than they actually are. The French 'archaeologist of the air,' Father Poidebard, who was among the first to make sensational discoveries from the air, found in his excavations in the Middle East that Roman town planners and military architects had simply incorporated earlier complexes of Assyrians, Babylonians, and Hittites into their plans, the latter having themselves already built on Stone Age constructions. This is also the case with the huge pyramids or temple platforms of the Americas, which, when they are dug into, reveal one or more inner pyramids, each of which has been covered over by the most recent one. In a sense, whole pages or entire chapters of human history may have been covered over in much the same way by newer races who did not deem it of interest to record the history of their predecessors and who simply used what was convenient of the older cultures and eventually forgot about them.

Great and powerful cities simply disappeared. In the case of Babylon, once a metropolis containing a population of millions, the very location was lost under the desert until it was rediscovered after 2000 years. Spina, a great maritime commercial city of the mysterious Etruscans, the pre-Roman rulers of Italy, was rediscovered only in 1935 from the air, almost by chance as the different shadings of growth pattern of coastal marshes traced the shape of ancient palaces, buildings, streets, and canals.

Other ancient cities that have been located such as Tiahuanaco in the Americas, Bronze Age centres of Northern Europe, deserted cities in the deserts of Central Asia, and the Indus Valley are lost to history in that there are no contemporary written records relating to them or at least no records we can read. The ancient Chaldeans left an ample time-space for prehistoric cultures, establishing a time lapse of exactly 39,180 years between the Deluge and the first historic dynasty.

We can only trace history when it is written and when dates can be ascribed to it; in the lack of written records cultures and civilizations remain permanently lost in a sea of conjecture and supposition, and thousands of years of prehistory exist only as legend legends in the memory of race or often are forgotten altogether. The term 'prehistoric' covers valuable history of the Stone and Bronze Ages, but unless it is recorded it remains, of course, prehistoric.

One prehistoric city that is still missing was nevertheless the subject of frequent ancient written comment; the semifabulous Tartessos on the west coast of Spain, reputedly near the present site of Cádiz. Although we have a tentative date for its conquest and destruction by the Carthaginians in 533 B.C. and numerous references to its wealth and prominence in Greek records, as well as the allusion to Tarshish (or Tartessos) in the Bible, the site of the city itself has not been located. It is thought to be either under the sea, under the mud of the Guadalquivir estuary, or even under the present streets of Seville. There are other cyclopean ruins at Niebla and Ronda, some of which were found after washout floods occurred in 1923, thought to be connected with the vanished Tartessos. Enormous harbor walls and stone staircases at nearby Huelva resemble the cyclopean masonry of the Incan Empire and its predecessors.

A highly interesting aspect of Tartessos or Tarshish is that it was located on the ocean of Spain and that it possessed an important merchant fleet at a very early date. The Bible, in describing the magnificence of Solomon's court, specifically mentions this trade in Kings 10:22: 'For the king had at sea a navy of Tharshish with the navy of Hiram; once in three years came the navy of Tharshish, bringing gold, and silver, ivory, and apes and peacocks.' And again in Ezekiel 27:12 we find: 'Tarshish was thy merchant by reason of the multitude of all kinds of riches, with silver, iron, tin and lead, they traded in thy fairs...' Early Greek records relate that ships that called at Tartessos found silver so plentiful that they substituted silver anchors for their leaden ones on the return trip.

The presence of this mercantile metropolis on the ocean side of Gibraltar has given rise to theories that Tartessos itself was Atlantis and that the Minoans and Greeks who visited there somehow projected the Atlantean legend on the rich and powerful city which did, in effect, 'disappear' after its conquest. The Carthaginians made doubly certain that this rich entrepôt would effectively disappear from view by making a treaty with Rome soon after its conquest, restricting oceanic travel outside Gibraltar to Carthaginian vessels alone.

This vanished culture of Tartessos was reputed to have used a written script in which the inhabitants kept records for thousands of years before its disappearance. Strabo, a Greek historian of the first century B.C. wrote: 'They are the most civilized of the Iberians. They know writing and have ancient books and also poems and laws in verse which they consider 7000 years old.' Incised inscriptions on rocks in Southwestern Spain, North Africa, and the Canary Islands show several scripts that seem to be alphabetic and not picture writing, resembling Phoenician or Etruscan, but which have not yet been deciphered and which may be related to that of Tartessos. An inscription on a ring found by a German professor near the supposed site of Tartessos shows a script that can be *pronounced* in Etruscan but is undecipherable for meaning.

The question of when the alphabet was invented is an intriguing one, since the alphabet itself, generally attributed to the Phoenicians, goes back only to the beginning of the second millennium B.C. This, of course does not mean that man did not write before that time but simply that he did not use an alphabet which would enable him to spell words using individual letters instead of pictures, as with the ancient Egyptian hieroglyphics and the Chinese ideographs, or a further simplification of hieroglyphics such as the cuneiform wedge writing of the Babylonians which represented complete syllables. Spelling by syllables is still effectively used in modern Japanese, Korean, and other scripts, but in general it is cumbersome because of the additional numbers of symbols needed and is not as effective as the true alphabet. The original Phoenician or North Semitic alphabet, from which all other true alphabets are descended, has been traced back to Byblos, Lebanon (cf. Bible, bibliography, bibliophile, etc.) where it was in use more than 4000 years ago.

The fact that Phoenician-type writing has been discovered in the western parts of the Mediterranean, the west coast of Spain, the islands of the Atlantic and the New World implies that the Phoenicians were not only great seafarers, which we already knew, but suggests as well that other African, Iberian, and Atlantic peoples were apparently using this alphabetical script to write their own languages. Many of the Phoenician-type inscriptions found in the Amazon and others discernible on rocks of the Atlantic islands and even the coast of the United States have long been branded hoaxes, although there exists the possibility that while the letters seem to be Phoenician, the language may be different.

Given the extreme age of Tartessos and the attributed antiquity of their writings as well as the undeciphered North African and Spanish inscriptions, one is led to contemplate the intriguing possibility that the Phoenicians did not develop the alphabet from the cuneiform and hieroglyphic sources at hand, but picked it up from a western source during their travels and adopted it initially as a useful shorthand of signal use in trade.

A most interesting theory on the origin of the alphabet is suggested by the work of Hugh Moran (*The Alphabet and the Ancient Calendar Signs*) and the research of Dr. Cyrus Gordon, author of numerous books on ancient Mediterranean culture and scripts. It is briefly that our alphabet came from the signs of the zodiac added to by signs for counting days in a lunar month.

The original alphabet or alphabets usually contained under thirty letters and were therefore influenced by the number of days in the month as well as the recurring zodiac and other constellations. Ancient seafarers would have needed an exact way of keeping count of days spent on voyages and may have designated and recorded numbers by simplified signs which also became an alphabet. It is known that, in the first alphabets, letters were used for counting as well as writing. In the case of Hebrew, an ancient language still very much alive, the numbers were expressed by the letters of the alphabet, alef, bet, gimmel, dalet, being 1, 2, 3, and 4. This can be noted today on some clocks and watches made in Israel which have Hebrew letters instead of having Roman or Arabic numerals to indicate the hours.

The mystery of the origin of the phonetic alphabet, therefore, may go back to an even older scientific attainment, that of counting, and the alphabet, if we follow the theory still further, may be the child of mathematics. The concept of the alphabet, or phonetic writing, was certainly an outstanding 'great step forward for mankind' to quote from Shepherd's contemporaneous comment on the first moon landing, without which we should certainly never have been able to store enough scientific facts to get to the moon. In like manner, this great scientific accomplishment was perhaps initiated untold thousands of years ago. The moon itself, whose phases started the first astrologers, astronomers, mathematicians or simply seafarers calculating cosmic time by the moon and subsequently by the moon count of days and nights and signs of

166

the circling zodiac forming a system of signs which developed into the alphabet.

The Phaistos Disk of Crete, a clay disk with what seems to be hieroglyphic figures imprinted in spirals on both sides. This disk may be a surviving example of the development of

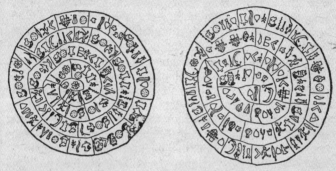

The Phaistos Disk, discovered in 1908 in Crete. It is not yet definitely known what the figures mean or whether they represent an alphabetical or hieroglyphic system of writing. There is an additional element of mystery in the fact that the figures were individually printed in the clay from seals—in other words, an ancient form of printing.

the alphabet through the zodiac if it is true, as has been suggested, that it uses zodiacal signs for phonetic symbols. Ever since the Phaistos Disk was discovered in 1908, philologists have been attempting to decipher it as a language text that could be 'broken' and subsequently translated. An authority on Minoan culture, Leon Pomerance, ventures the opinion that it is not written in a language at all, but it is an allusive system of allegorical symbols, stemming from the constellations of the zodiac, as well as other constellations, which are to be 'interpreted' but not translated, and when correctly understood, make an invocation or hymn to the sun. One of the recurring figures on the disk is a head which appears to be wearing a feather headdress, a curiosity that has suggested transatlantic influence to some views and Atlantean references to others. Other signs on the Phaistos Disk recur in other carvings on monuments in Crete and other islands in the Aegean and the Mediterranean and on another larger spiral legend carved on a round stone in Dendera, Egypt.

A striking feature of the Phaistos Disk is that the different symbols were impressed individually on the wet clay, another way of saying that the Phaistos Disk was printed using movable type some thousands of years before printing was invented. However it is true that signatory seals, a form of printing, often circular, to be rolled on, were widely used in antiquity from the very earliest cultures in Egypt, Sumeria, the Indus Valley, and other places; the extraordinary aspect of the Phaistos Disk being that a collection of recurring seals or symbols was used to form a more complete text. In a word, the principle of printing by type was known in very early times, but whether it was ever used on papyrus, stones, or a substance like paper will doubtlessly remain a mystery to us.

The beginning of writing of any sort, whether markings carved or notched on reindeer or other bones, painted or carved in stone, incised in clay, or painted on walls of caves, is constantly being revised backward into time. Writing as such should not be considered pictured scenes but simply the marks or symbols, perhaps coming originally from pictures, to convey concrete or abstract ideas.

Some such inscriptions have been found in Western Europe, of such great age that it is considered that, although the objects are genuine, they cannot be writing. A piece of reindeer bone from a cave at Rochebertier, France, seems to contain some symbols resembling the unknown inscription of the ring from Tartessos, while antlers from other caves at Mas d'Azil and La Madeleine are also inscribed with signs resembling Phoenician letters. At this same site the famous Mas d'Azil painted pebbles have been found in quantity. Some of these colored pebbles seem to have letters on them, although it is possible that the apparent letters may be symbols, totem marks, counting marks, or simply designs, although design for design's sake would be as remarkable in a sense as the other purposes attributed to the Azilian pebbles. One of the pebbles bears the circled cross, a design frequently appearing, like the swastika, at widely separated parts of the world and, again like the swastika, used as a symbol of life force and divinity many thousands of years before its temporary conversion to a symbol of nationalism and race—the swastika in Germany and the circled or 'Celtic' cross in France.

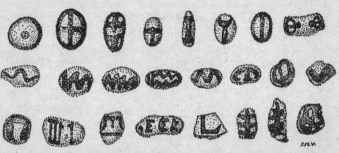

Examples of Azilian pebbles. These painted pebbles from the prehistoric Magdalenian age have been thought to be a form of writing or perhaps the ancestor of writing. Recent investigations, however, imply that a form of astronomical notation, itself a form of writing, existed in Crô-Magnon times, as early as 30,000 years ago.

Even more remarkable are the larger 'alphabet' finds of Glozel unearthed in 1924 near Vichy, France, and the subject of acrimonious debate ever since. Among bricks, axes, pottery, and tablets of the Magdalenian era, one incised tablet in particular, part of the general find, shows a collection of signs or letters, several of which are equivalent to Phoenician or Greek, while others are unidentifiable. Clearly defined writing of this era and in such a location is archaeologically unacceptable and, although the Glozel tablets have been vouched for by many prehistorians, the mystery still stands. A mystery which, if verified, would indicate that unknown people in Northern Europe were able to write thousands of years before the Egyptians first developed their hieroglyphic script—a most unsettling concept to traditional archaeology.

A further unorthodox theory concerning prehistoric writing, this time still further back, from the older Aurignacian era was made public in 1971 by Alexander Marshack, an anthropological researcher, who has taken a longer look at some of the eagle, mammoth, and deer bones found in Aurignacian caves, now kept in various museums throughout

A tablet from Glozel, France, also from Magdalenian times, with clearly marked letters of some sort. This tablet, although vouched for by many authorities of prehistory, has been attacked as spurious, possibly because its acceptance as authentic would imply a sweeping re-evaluation of established theories.

Europe, and advanced the opinion that searchers, notches, and incisions on these bones were a selection of markings that served as a calendar adjusted to the moon with modified notations, cut with a variety of tools, which would be equivalent to a primitive form of writing or at least record keeping by carved notations. This would put written notation, if not writing, back about 30,000 years.

These markings had previously been noticed on these prehistoric bones but had been attributed to decorations or incisions on the handle of a probable tool for the purpose of securing a better grip. Alexander Marshack, in noting a series of varying symbols resembling differing crescentations of the moon and a system of notched straight lines, as if they were checked off, deduced the theory of a lunar calendar and checked other museum pieces, sometimes using special lighting and high magnification to bring out the true shapes of the markings. He often found animal or woman figures mixed in with the apparent calendar notations, the latter suspected of possible connections with hunting for game or recording the female menstrual cycle.

Indications of such an important step toward civilization as the beginnings of writing as early as 35,000 years ago, when writing had previously been considered no older than five or six thousand years at the very most, would leave a considerable time space for the development of prehistoric cultures of which we presently gave only vague indications. It can, of course, be argued that true civilization could not start without the cultivation of crops and the domestication of animals, but this figure too has been pushed back several thousand years from the traditional starting point of Sumeria. Cultivated plants have already been traced back 11,000 to 12,000 years and future discoveries will probably bring about future modification backward.

The concept of lost ages of civilization, of advanced cultures so far back in the past that they do not fit in any previously established pattern of civilization, is naturally looked upon with skepticism, suspicion, and sometimes alarm by the scientific and archaeological establishment. This is understandable at a time when archaeological artifacts have occasionally been attributed to visitors from other planets in our own solar system, such as Venus or Mars, or from planets in other solar systems. An understandable desire on the part of experts to keep things within their established boundaries, however, does not mean that new information will not basically alter previous concepts. This has happened many times before in recorded history in the case of the acceptance of scientific theories or inventions, a process which may reflect within the period of our own human race, here on this planet, the flux and reflux of civilization itself.

CHAPTER TEN

THE LONG MEMORY OF RACE

Throughout the world there are certain legends or traditions so similar in basic content that it is hard to believe that they did not have a common origin. The most dramatic is the flood legend, concerning the wickedness of a prediluvian civilization that God or the gods, depending on the tradition, decided to destroy, in each case selecting one man, one couple, or more, as survivors and warning them before the catastrophe. Our own Judeo-Christian tradition of Noah and the ten generations before him perhaps comes from or is related to a similar Babylonian legend and so is the Islamic tradition where the destroyed people are called—somewhat coincidentally for Atlantologists—'the people of Ad.' The Great Flood and subsequent repopulation of the earth by chosen survivors was known to all the peoples of antiquity—in Greece and the Mediterranean world, the tribes of Northern Europe, long before Christianity made its appearance, as well as in Sumeria, Babylon, Persia, India, China, and other parts of Asia. This widespread legend was even found to be well distributed among the Amerind population of the New World, with some modifications of how the survivors escaped and the animals chosen to be saved adapted to the American locale, such as llamas, buffaloes, jaguars, coyotes, and others according to place. Sometimes even the number of days it rained almost coincides on both sides of the Atlantic, varying from the biblical forty days and nights to sixty in some of the Amerind versions.

The prevalence of these flood legends, as well as high water marks on plateaus and mountains throughout the world including traces of marine life in the Himalayas and a 'marine bed' between culture levels in ancient Mesopotamia, imply that one or several floods or great rising of the waters with accompanying tidal waves occurred and was witnessed by survivors who kept the story alive through legend and eventual transcription down to the present time. And, if one or more land masses became submerged at such a time, survivors of what must have been numerous islands, landing in different parts of the world, must have thought or at least told the semibarbaric people they came in contact with that they were the only survivors of the catastrophe; in other words, there were many 'Noahs.'

There seems to be no linguistic connection between the names of the survivors of the flood with that of Noah of Judeo-Christian-Islamic tradition. In Babylonian legend he was Ut-Napishtam; Yima in ancient Iran; Deucalion in Greco-Roman legend; Baisbasbata in Hindu mythology; Coxcox or Tezpi in Aztec and pre-Aztec legend; and Tamandaré in the Guarani legends of Brazil, Paraguay, and Argentina.

The huge pyramid of Cholula in Mexico was reportedly constructed so that the builders would have a place of refuge to escape another flood, but was said to have been abandoned by its builders before it had reached its projected height because of a confusion of languages. This last instance of legends, such as the Tower of Babel, crossing oceans contributed to the Spanish priests' belief that Satan was somehow in back of the extraordinary coincidences that were probably meant to confuse true believers. These coincidences included the sculptured crosses throughout ancient Mexico, the crosses on the robe of Quetzalcóatl, the existence of confession, fasting, penance, and forgiveness of sins in the Aztec religion, along with the distinctly un-Christian ritual of human sacrifice.

As customs, legends, and stories could easily spread across Europe and Asia and across the Mediterranean to Africa, true diffusion of what may be culture patterns could be most profitably searched for in the isolated parts of the world, remote islands in both the oceans and comparatively remote continents, such as the Americas. Culture patterns and shared memories between such isolated places and other parts of the world suggest that they were perhaps not so isolated in pre-historic times, using the word prehistoric in the sense of before history as we have recorded it. People and races tend to remember things for a variety of reasons. They remember what they have found useful, what is amusing, diverting, or beautiful, and also what has caused them to experience terror and awe.

The use of cotton in ancient America falls into this 'useful' category but contains elements of mystery, principally, as Constance Irwin observes in her book *Fair Gods and Stone Faces*, because of the chromosome count. Wild cotton in America had thirteen small chromosomes and cotton from the ancient world had thirteen large chromosomes. But cotton found at Huaca Prieta, one of the oldest sites dated in Peru (2347 B.C.), had thirteen small and thirteen large chromosomes, presumably resulting from the hybridization of Old World and American cotton thousands of years ago. Moreover, the looms used for weaving cotton in Peru were almost identical with those of ancient Egypt, even to the point of each having eleven working parts. According to Thor Heyerdahl's theory, such exchanges came from East to West, although there exists the possibility that both areas benefited from a common, more central source.

In ancient Mexico the Spanish invaders found that the Aztecs played a game (while they still had time for games, before the advent of the Spaniards) which was exactly the same as *parchesi*, played thousands of years ago in India and Persia, except that in Mexico marked beans were used instead of dice. The Aztecs called it *patolli*, a name vaguely reminiscent, but had no record of who invented it or on what ships it crossed the Pacific if, effectively, that was the ocean it crossed to come to Mexico.

Sometimes the most unlikely source will point to contact between the isolated New World and the 'older' continents. As an example consider a simple story told by the Irish in the Old World and the Ojibway Indians in pre-Columbian America, corresponding in almost every detail but still dissimilar from and older than the usual European folk tales:

Ojibway Indian Legend: The birds met together one day to try which could fly the highest. Some flew up very swift, but soon got tired, and were passed by others of stronger wing. But the eagle went up beyond them all, and was ready to claim the victory, when the gray linnet, a small small bird, flew from the eagle's back, where it had perched unperceived, and, being fresh and unexhausted, succeeded in going the highest. When the birds came down and met in council to award the prize, it was given to the eagle, because the bird had not only gone up nearer to the sun than any of the larger birds, but had carried the linnet on its back.

For this reason the eagle's feathers became the most honorable marks of distinction a warrior could bear.

Gaelic Folk Tale: The birds all met together one day, and settled among themselves that whichever of them could fly highest was to be the king of all. Just as they were about to be off a wren perched himself unbeknown on the eagle's tail. So they flew and flew ever so high, till the eagle was miles above all the rest, and could not fly another stroke, he was so tired. 'Then,' says he, 'I'm king of the birds.' 'You lie!' says the wren, darting up a perch and a half above the big bird. Well, the eagle was so angered ... that when the wren was coming down he gave him a stroke of his wing, and from that day to this the wren was never able to fly farther than a hawthorn bush.

Harold Sterling Gladwin in his book *Men out of Asia* underscores a seemingly minor musical element in former Old World contacts with America; the panpipes, a musical instrument of aligned tubes or reeds played by the god Pan and the shepherds of ancient Greece, have been found of almost identical manufacture in the Solomon Islands of the Pacific and the highlands of the Andes, where shepherds still play them to llamas and sheep and where they also are an integral part of the lively indigenous music. Besides the structural resemblance, even the pitch of these panpipes has been found

175

to be the same in these points half a world apart.

In ascribing extensive ancient contacts with the Americas from other parts of the world, one must exercise a certain caution in recognizing simple designs carved or incised on stone or metal or painted on pottery or woven in cloth, since many symbolic figures for man, animals, the sun, moon, and stars, mountains, and parts of the human anatomy are generally drawn in more or less the same fashion simply because that

Striking similarity is shown between art motifs of China and Mexico in the two decorative borders shown above, the upper coming from the early Ch'ou Dynasty in China and the lower from El Tajin, Mexico. The similarities, including the use of the double line for emphasis and the curved 'tiger tufts' at the bottom are too exact to be fortuitous.

is the easiest and most natural way to draw them. Occasionally, however, one finds a design of such intricacy that its presence in two widely separated places would be outside the bounds of coincidental probability. Such an example can be seen in the 'Chinese' frieze motifs found at El Tajín and outer sites in Mexico, when they are compared with extremely ancient designs from China from the earliest dynasties, such as the Hsia, Shang, and Chou (2000 to 250 B.C.).

Another surprising coincidental design is that of the labyrinth or maze found among Indian cultures of North and

176

South America, in Egyptian tombs, and in ancient Crete where it was given such importance that it was even struck on early Cretan coins. In Greek legend the labyrinth was literally the cage for the terrible minotaur, the man-bull, a primitive interpretation of its real use, probably connected with religious ceremonies as were the pre-Cretan tomb labyrinths of ancient Egypt, allegorically connected with the wanderings of the soul after death.

Labyrinth design used in pre-Columbian Ecuador (left) compared with two labyrinth patterns traditionally employed by the Hopi Indians. Other designs showing labyrinths appear throughout the Mediterranean, especially centered in the Minoan civilization of ancient Crete, with its fearsome legend of the Minotaur.

Racial memories of other cultures and buildings or monuments that have since disappeared may be the explanation for relatively primitive tribes repeating designs and even buildings in constantly receding patterns of civilization once the initial impetus has been lost. This is what may have occurred with the gigantic statues of Easter Island, Rapa Itu, the stone structures of the Carolines and Marianas, the huge stone figures in New Guinea, endlessly repeated by the otherwise acultural Malekula tribe in honour of their 'ancestor,' the stone forts of Ireland and the Aran Islands, the megalithic stonework of the Mediterranean Islands, Portugal and southern Spain, the thousands of carefully aligned menhirs at Carnac in Brittany, Stonehenge, and Avebury in England and the unexplained prehistoric buildings on the coasts and waterways of both Americas.

But there is another stronger tie of racial memory—the memory of language. It is interesting to consider that the spoken sounds of language, one of the most ephemeral and easily modified means of communication, has been preserved through uncounted generations, antedating our most ancient written records, and in the case of some languages, coming down more or less directly from prehistoric times to the present.

In the intellectual ferment of the nineteenth century, when prehistory and man's origins were first subjected to scientific scrutiny, many languages, ancient and modern, were compared for common meanings, roots, and construction for the purpose of indicating a common origin, perhaps to find the basic language of man before the fabled or allegorical incident at the Tower of Babel. Almost all the languages of Europe and some of those of the Middle East as far as India are connected, both through vocabulary and construction; they probably are descended from a parent language beyond history which has given common features to them all. German linguists originally classified all these languages as Indo-Germanic, although we generally tend to use the more neutral term of French linguists—Indo-European.

In tracing the antiquity and origin of Indo-European languages it has been suggested that the parent language may have started in Europe in the vicinity of the Rhine, Oder, Elbe, and Vistula rivers principally because of the prevalence of a set of three words in this language group and no other: 'turtle,' 'beech tree,' and 'salmon'—all of which existed in the geographical boundaries of the above European rivers. Because of its geographical proximity to the Indo-European or Indo-Germanic language group, the Semitic languages of the Middle East and to a lesser extent the Turkic languages of Central Asia, often have shared word origins, to a much greater extent, until modern times, than with the Semitic language group of the Far East, the hundreds of languages of Sub-Sahara Africa, the tongues of the Pacific islands, and the more than one thousand Amerind languages which, if Columbus was the first contact between America and the rest of the world, should have no words at all in common with the languages of Europe and Asia.

It is therefore no longer a surprising phenomenon to find essentially the same word existing in a variety of modern and ancient Indo-European languages since the great tribal migration spread the Indo-European languages throughout Europe and a large part of Asia. What would be most unusual, therefore, would be to find words or influences from other recognizable languages in the Amerind languages or in other linguistic islands of isolation in the world, indicating that at some time, several thousands of years ago, a sea culture or cultures may have spread elements of language as well as civilization to far places on the shores of the oceans.

The recurrent legend of the Tower of Babel on both sides of the ocean may be a common memory of the disappearance of an older language, not necessarily spoken as a native tongue by divergent peoples, but generally used as a vehicle of culture and trade, as is the case today with the use of English in Asia and Africa, and other international languages spoken by 'second users' such as French, Russian, Spanish, Arabic, and, more recently, Malay and Swahili.

Perhaps the disappearance of a language or languages formerly widely used in world communication between peoples, and the subsequent realization that such a vehicle was no longer available, gave rise to the curious legend of the Tower of Babel, making of it a sort of linguistic monument to the vanished tongue.

Sometimes the loss of a common language is noted in legends without reference to the Tower.

The Mayan *Popul Vuh*, compiled from the original Maya records, contains the following:

Those who gazed at the rising of the sun ... had but one language ... This occurred after they had arrived at Tulán, before going West. Here the language of the tribes was changed. Their speech became different. All that they had heard and understood when departing from Tulán had become incomprehensible to them...

and again:

> For the tongue(s) ... had already become different.
> ... Alas, alas, we have abandoned our speech! Why did
> we do this? ... Our language was one when we departed
> from Tulán, one in the country where we were born...'

The lack of any usable bridge language with their conquerors was one more disadvantage to the Indian civilizations
of Central America for, if they had known from the beginning
what the Spanish planned for them the history of the New
World might well have been different. When the Spanish
conquistadors came into contact with the Indians of Mexico
for the first time they generally addressed them in Latin, and
later sometimes in Greek, since some of the Maya syllables
sounded more like Greek than Latin. Some unusual incidents
occurred—when the Spaniards in Yucatán asked the leader of
a Maya group in Latin what their land was called the chief
replied 'Yucatán?' (What did you say?), and this word was
duly set down as the name of the territory. On another occasion, a Spanish soldier was about to kill an Indian who unexpectedly said in Spanish 'Do not slay me, *cabellero*. I am a
Castillian like yourself.' He was telling the truth, having been
shipwrecked some time ago, and now a slave of the Maya.
When he rejoined his countrymen he was a most useful in-
terpreter with the Mayas and, through his knowledge of the
Maya language, with the Aztecs.

As they became more familiar with the Indian languages,
the Spanish priests began to find what they considered Greek
and Hebrew and even Basque words mixed in with the native
languages, not only in Central America but even in Peru.
These coincidences were variously interpreted as due to such
probabilities as the Indians being the ten lost tribes of Israel
or descendants of the Atlanteans; both of which being considered an additional reason for conquest and conversion by
the Spanish conquerors. Several of the words noted at this
early period are strangely coincidental—the Náhuatl (Aztec)
word or word prefix for 'god' or 'gods' is *teotl* shortened to

téo in compound words (*theos* is 'god' in Greek), and often occurs in combinations such as *teocalli*—'house of the god' (Kalía is 'small dwelling' in Greek), *Teotl* (*téo*) is also used in many place names, such as the famous pyramids of Teotihuacan (literally 'the place of those who have the gods'). The curious double coincidence of the resemblance of *teocalli* to *theou kalías*—'dwelling of god' in ancient Greek caused Alexander von Humboldt, an earlier student of the Aztecs, to exclaim: 'This is pure Greek!'—a somewhat overenthusiastic statement, albeit understandable under the circumstances.

The Aymará language of the Andean Highlands used the word *mallku* for 'king,' reminiscent of the Hebrew *melek* or the Arabic *malik*; while the word *garúa* ('drizzle') was the same in Quechua, the imperial language of the Incas, and Basque. A Mayan exorcism was found to resemble almost exactly a phrase used in the ancient secret celebration of the Greek mysteries. The name of Tlaloc, the Mexican rain and water god, has been compared with the Greek word for 'sea' —*thalassa*—not only for the sound of the name but for the element which he rules. Even in the United States we have what may be simply a linguistic chance—the resemblance between the name of our famous river, the Potomac, with the Greek word for 'river,' *potomos*.

In examining languages or groups of languages for affinities with others one must be careful not to jump to conclusions because of certain chance resemblances, unless, of course, they are often repeated. The English adverb and interjection 'so,' for example, is used in almost exactly the same way in Japanese. The English word 'hole' is represented by the same sound in Maya. The fact that 'so' was a Japanese word before contact with the outside world is a 'linguistic chance'; but the fact that Japanese now contains 2000 or more adopted English words is sufficient to indicate to archaeologists of the future an important cultural contact. Therefore, for purposes of identifying ancient contacts with the Americas, caution should also be exercised to avoid *new* words, possibly adopted wholesale into Indian languages from the languages of the discoverers. In this regard one is linguistically safer when examining basic

181

words, designations of things that are constant to a given culture, then names of animals, birds, foods, family and tribal relationships, and natural or supernatural phenomena—and also in considering languages already ancient or having disappeared at the time of the discovery of America or the mid-Pacific islands.

Besides the influence of ancient Greek, curious imports from other older cultures appear in words of the New World. *Tepe* means 'hill' in the Turkic languages of Central Asia, and a similar word—*tepetl* or *tepec*—means 'hill' in Aztec (Náhuatl) as in Chapul*tepec*—'Hill of the Grasshopper,' and Popoca*tepetl*—'Smoking Mountain,' in Egypt the crocodile, sacred in ancient tmies, was called *s-b-k* (we do not know the exact value of the vowels) and in Náhuatl *cipac-tli*. The Latin *papilio*—'butterfly'—appears in Náhuatl as *papalo-tl,* and even a word resembling the extremely ancient Sumerian word for 'antelope'—*mash*—appears in Náhuatl as the word for 'deer'—*mazatl*—which the Aztecs called the Spanish horses, not knowing what else to call them. In Maya, the word for 'priest' is *balaam*, while *bileam* means 'magician' in Hebrew.

Striking similarities occur in the languages of even minor tribes. The Phoenician name for the Sun God was *Shapash*, and *shapash* means 'the sun' among the Klamath, an Indian tribe of northern California and southern Oregon. In the Hopi language the Sun God is called *Taiowa*, while 'the sun' (as subject) is *taiyo-wa* in Japanese. *Kharus*—'gold' in Phoenician; *cuarasi* is the word for 'sun' in the Guarani language of southeastern South America. These words have a resemblance that becomes even closer when we consider that in South America gold was the metal associated with the sun, being referred to by the Incas as the 'tears of the sun.' Quechua, the former court and administrative language of the Inca Empire, and still spoken by millions of Indians in the Andean Plateau, has been attributed affinities with such widely separated languages as Basque and Japanese. Both of these resemble Quechua in some of its syllables and Basque in its construction, since they are both agglutinitive languages but, former picturesque reports to the contrary, Japanese and Quechua or

182

Basque and Quechua are not mutually understandable, although some words are surprisingly alike, albeit with different meanings. Basque, which may antedate the other languages of Europe, has no ties with any of them except for a small language pocket in the Caucasus Mountains, and follows the agglutinative language pattern of Quechua and other Amerind languages. In addition, Quechua seems to have specific words in common with islands of the Pacific, especially with the Maori language of New Zealand and even the languages of Malaya and India.

Common words between Quechua and Maori are convincing examples of cultural contacts via ocean voyages across the Pacific.

MAORI:

Muna (Love)	*Nocu* (My)	*Kiri* (Skin)	*Mutu* (Mutilated)	*Pura* (Between)	*Kura* (Chieftain)	*Kumara* (Sweet Potato)

QUECHA:

Munay (Love)	*Nuca* (I)	*Kara* (Skin)	*Mutu* (Mutilated)	*Pura* (Between)	*Kuraca* (Chieftain)	*Kumara* (Sweet Potato)

Other surprising vestiges of vanished languages appear in Quechua—the word for 'lie' (untruth) is *llullu* in Quechua and *lul* in ancient Sumerian; 'reeds' are *sug* in Sumerian and *soco* in Quechua, while the Quechua word for 'basket'— *kusuru*—has essentially the same consonants as the Sumerian *kasher*. Sometimes the similarity between words such as the Babylonian *laklak* for 'big bird' and the Quechua *lleka-lleka* for 'heron' may be simply examples of onomatopoeia, or words expressing the sound of an action, in this case, the flapping of the big bird's wings.

Even more striking are the word similarities between Hawaiian and ancient Greek which appear to indicate that seafarers, speaking ancient Greek or a similar language, sailed an ocean that, as far as we know, the Greeks of history did not even know existed. A list compiled by Arnold Wadler (*One Language*) includes the following words of common sound and meaning, considering the tendency for simplification on the part of the melodious Tahitian-Hawaiian language:

HAWAIIAN:

| Aeto (Eagle) | Noo-Noo (Thought) | Manao (Think) | Mele (Sing) | Lahui (People) | Hiki (Come) | Noko (Live, sit) |

ANCIENT GREEK:

| Aetos (Eagle) | Nous (Intelligence) | Manthano (Learn) | Melodhia (Melody) | Laos (People) | Hikano (Arrive) | Naio (Dwell) |

What happened to the records of such world circling by Minoan, Greek, or Phoenician fleets? It is probable that many were lost in the frequent conquest and destruction of books and records in the Phoenician cities and the final obliteration of Carthage by the Romans. Just one mention has come down to us, that of a rather leisurely trip around Africa by Phoenicians in the employ of the Egyptian Pharaoh Necho, starting from the Red Sea at a time when the former 'Suez' canal from the Gulf of Suez to the Nile and the Mediterranean was no longer usable. (A strange preview of the present!) Probably the only reason that this particular trip is known to us is because it was sponsored by the Egyptian Empire, and was included in Egyptian records. The Phoenicians themselves habitually and assiduously kept their voyages and trade routes secret from possible competitors, with mandatory death penalty for violators of such state secrets.

It is also possible that the fleets that left vestiges of culture and language over the world did not come from the centers we usually associate with Greeks and Phoenicians but from other earlier lands now lost, of which there remains only an imperfect and diminishing echo of language and cultures in isolated islands and unexpected coasts. We will probably never know whether these seafarers spoke a form of Greek, Phoenician, Sumerian, Basque, Maya, Quechua, or more likely, a parent language or languages which has left traces in all languages from the days when the oceans were lower, islands were larger and there were more of them, and before climatic changes and seismic upheavals modified whole sections of the world and destroyed or scattered its population.

The fleets that spread civilization and culture over the oceans and coasts of the world before history have long since vanished, although some vessels may yet be found preserved under ice, coral, the sands of the sea bottom, or the mud of a silted-up estuary, or even under the very deep and preserving muck of the ocean bottom. Memories of this culture diffusion are suggested only by certain words in other languages, washed up from somewhere like flotsam on a beach, preserved in racial memory through millennia by the persistence of spoken language.

Even a rather unusual place name will appear in different parts of the world, as if a new city were named for an old one, like New York for York and the many European names of American cities named in honour of their predecessors. This may be the case of Carnac, in Brittany, with its thousands of stone menhirs standing in rows by the sea and Karnak in Egypt with its rows of enormous temple columns. Another ancient city, called Kanarak exists in southern India, still others as in Scotland, where there are two, both spelled Carnock. Among other name resemblances, there is a Kanak in Turkey, a Kanayka in the Kazakh S.S.R., a Carna in Ireland, a Carnaxide in Portugal, some of which may refer to an older similar sounding city. Carthage, the ancient metropolis of North Africa, may possibly be related to the Kar of Karnak since *kart* in Phoenician meant 'city' or 'town.' A similar word for 'town'—*car*—appears in South America among the Araucanian Indians and again in Brittany where the word for 'town' is *ker*.

The place name Tula occurs in western Ireland and in eastern Mexico, where it is not only the name of an actual place but also the legendary home of Quetzalcóatl in the Eastern Sea. The Roman designation of Thule may have referred to one of the Hebrides Islands or even Iceland, and the phrase Ultima Thule given on some of the old Latin maps was meant to indicate the western end of the earth. The word Tula or Thule forms a great triangle around the ocean, much as the different names for Atlantis form a great clockwise circle from Venezuela through Mexico, Central America, Yucatán, and the Antilles to Europe, eastward to the Méditerranean and North Africa and westward again to the Canary Islands. This

185

'word memory' of Atlantis or the most important component letters A-T-L-N, preserved by so many tribes and nations around the perimeter of the Atlantic Ocean, is perhaps the most striking linguistic race memory of all, and the regional variations of the name serve to make it only more convincing.

The Guanches of the Canary Islands preserved an oral and written tradition for thousands of years of an event that sounds like a corroboration of Plato's story of Atlantis. When the first Spanish navigators reached the Canary Islands in the fourteenth century they found remnants of an advanced, well-organized Stone Age culture, including such 'Atlantean' elements as stone buildings, a written script, sun worship, mummies, bull fights, and even ten elected kings, reminiscent of the Ten Kings of Atlantis mentioned by Plato and the Ten Kings of the Maya. When the Guanches were able to communicate with the Spaniards they expressed surprise that people other than themselves had survived the catastrophe of their former much larger homeland. In effect, however, the final catastrophe for the Guanches transpired with the arrival of the Spaniards. When the smoke cleared, the records and language of the Guanches had disappeared, along with most of the population. Among the Guanche words that have survived, several basic words, such as 'god,' 'sun,' and 'moon,' have an intriguing similarity to figures of Greek mythology. The Guanche word for 'god' was *coron*, which resembles *chronos*—the Titan who ruled the Universe and whose name has long figured in the Atlantean legend. The Guanche word for 'sun' was *alio* and the word for 'moon' *sel*, corresponding rather closely with the Greek sun god *Aelios* or *Helios* and the moon goddess *Selene*. Research of prehistoric Atlantic culture would be greatly furthered if more elements of the Guanche language could be developed and studied. Some shepherd communities in the mountains of Gran Canaria are reported to have retained a certain purity of race and even to have preserved some of their ancient language, but are unenthusiastic, like so many primitive survivors, at being interviewed about their past culture. Investigation of the Guanche language and its possible connections with Basque, Berber, ancient Egyptian, and the mysterious

Temanagh, the language of the isolated Tuareg tribe of the Sahara might lead to some linguistic and cultural surprises.

Inherited instinct or the retained memory of species, which may be the same thing, has frequently been brought into consideration as an indication of former land masses or a submerged continent in the Atlantic. This category includes the suicidal migrations of the lemmings from Norway, when hordes of these small rodents enter the sea and swim westward, as if they were in search of a land, the memory of which they have possibly *inherited*, until the drown.

Another observed phenomenon concerns the seasonal flights of birds across the ocean from Europe to South America, during which some flocks circle aimlessly over spots in mid-ocean, as if looking for land, and then proceed after some of the flock have fallen into the sea.

On the Pacific side of South America we find what may be a remarkable instance of nostophylia—reluctance to abandon the ancestral home—occurring in the Andean Plateau, the only place in the world where flamingoes inhabit a high mountain range, but fly to the lowlands of the Pacific coast to feed. Possibly retaining a memory of the Andean Plateau *before* it was raised to its present height (the saline lakes and marshes on the summit Andean plateaus from Peru to Chile possess clear indications of swift orogenic uplift of marine beds), the flamingoes continue to live in what is at present a most inclement climate for flamingoes as well as one deficient in food.

The most intriguing of all is the spawning migration of the European eels, a mystery first mentioned by Aristotle in antiquity. The eels do not spawn in Europe but cross the Atlantic in a great moving bank of eels, to the Sargasso Sea where the spawning takes place. The Sargasso, while exactly fulfilling the qualification of being 'the sea of lost ships,' where, through the ages, ships have been entrapped and immobilized by clinging seaweed, is nevertheless a sea within the ocean, characterized by much seaweed. It is located west of the Atlantic Ridge, roughly circled by the Gulf Stream, the Bermuda Islands being the only land within its area. To students of Atlantis, naturally, the constant presence of seaweed is as intriguing as the 'racial memory' of the eels in that it suggests suddenly submerged verdant forests, vestiges of which are still growing in the sea or beneath it.

If it is conceivable that animals might inherit memory, how much more probable it would be for a more highly developed species like the human race to inherit memory patterns along with other physical, mental, and emotional characteristics. The storage facilities and the extent of storage of the human brain is still largely a mystery—there are large 'silent' areas of the brain, frequently calculated as 90 percent or more, of as yet undetermined use. Unidentified neuronal pathways lead to what might be called a memory bank with which the most complicated computer could not compare. The memory of an individual is classified as anthrogenetic—the memory of one's own experiences—while the philogenetic memory refers to the memory that may come from one's ancestors, in other words, a memory of race. Such studies of the contents and memory patterns in the brain are still in early and undeveloped stages, although it is conceivable, as suggested by legends and records, that in other earlier cultures such research, bordering on the para-physical, were more advanced.

If it were possible to tap from selected individuals part of this protoplasmic memory stream inherited from past generations, individual experiences, put in their proper time era, could presumably constitute an additional way of researching history. This would also furnish a fairly logical explanation of some of the more startling examples of reincarnation wherein children spoke in languages which they could not possibly have learned, or individuals remembered, through dreams or under hypnosis, details of lives and complete events of past eras, which, when in a conscious state, they knew nothing about.

In any case, what appears to be the fantasy or imaginative theoretization of today has often turned out to be the scientific fact of tomorrow, and eventually the long memory of race may prove to retain considerably more than inherited language, customs, and colorful legends.

Except in the case of Hinduism or Buddhism we hear very

little of human beings being reincarnated from animals, birds, or fish. Almost all of the mysterious reincarnation cases of recent times have dealt with people being reincarnated from people, and not always of the same sex. To a casual observer this seems understandable, inasmuch as we are all 'reincarnated' in the lateral sense of the word, from our own parents and our ancestors before them. And, as long as our descendants conserve certain physical characteristics, instincts, preferences, and even memory capsules, our ancestors, and we too, will continue a 'reincarnated' existence, even though nations and cultures may change or vanish.

CHAPTER ELEVEN

THE SHAKINGS OF THE WORLD

What sort of cataclysm was it that was severe enough to change the surface of the earth, decimate its human and animal populations, change its climate zones, push up mountains, raise some lands from the sea bottom and sink other lands beneath the ocean? Was it a gradual change or did it transpire like the coming of doom, killing men and animals by the millions and obliterating entire civilizations? At present we do not know what happened: we have only theories. The theories and associated inferences of gradual change and cataclysmic change had been (and still is being) debated by geologists, paleontologists, prehistorians and astronomers with a faith and bitterness worthy of the religious wars of the Middle Ages, of which, of course, they may be a modern counterpart.

Notwithstanding the relative values of the theories of gradual terrestrial modification and catastrophic planet-wide destruction, certain evidences that have long been at hand seem to give a certain credence to the latter. Early Russian explorers of northern Siberia found inexplicable masses of bones of elephants, rhinoceroses, and other non-Arctic animals wedged so close together that they formed hills on the land and underwater ledges on northern islands. Mammoths in deep-freeze have been found in Siberia from the nineteenth century onward (one was recently found in May 1971 near the Indigirka River), some with their eyeballs still in place and with plant food in their stomachs—plants that have not grown in Siberia since it has had a sub-Arctic or Arctic climate. Some mammoths still had half-chewed grasses on their tongues. (No evergreens have been found in the stomachs of mammoths; only grasses from temperate climates.) Other mammoths have been found in an instant-frozen condition, their meat, when defrosted, still suitable for human consumption, being first tested on sledge dogs. Some mammoths have been found frozen in blocks of ice, giving rise to legends, probably by hunters who so saw them, that mammoths are still living in Siberia. When the mammoths did live in Siberia and Alaska, however, the climate was considerably warmer, and whatever catastrophe trapped them and subsequently froze them was obviously a sudden one. One mammoth was found at 66° latitude, Siberia, near the Arctic Circle, as its head became exposed during a landslide. There was half-chewed food in its mouth but its bones had been suddenly broken, apparently immediately before its death. Another specimen was found with buttercups (no longer local flora) still in its mouth, a rather touching but effective proof of a sudden change in climate.

Mammoths and mastodons were apparently exterminated quickly along with a variety of other animals. Among animals found in the asphalt pits of La Brea, near Los Angeles, California, were hundreds of saber-tooth tigers, horses, camels, mammoths, mastodons, bison, and peacocks, all apparently suddenly caught in some sudden doom. Almost identical phenomena have been noted in many different sections of the world. A hill near Chalon-sur-Saône, France, has produced an unusual concentration of bones of mammals—rhinoceroses, horses, bears, lions, deer, and smaller animals. In the words of Professor Albert Gaudry: 'It is not possible to suppose that animals of such different natures, and of such different habits would in life have ever been together.'—a suggestion that common danger during a cataclysm had temporarily dissolved the boundaries between the hunted and the hunters.

An odd corroboration of the almost instantaneous destruction of animal life comes from the East Asian art of ivory carving practiced in China for thousands of years. Ivory that is used for fine carvings must be relatively fresh; if it lies out in the weather it becomes brittle and cracks. The ivory used for much of the ancient Chinese carvings was excavated from 'ivory mines' of Asia and Siberia where mammoths had been frozen quickly and preserved by the cold or mud slides that had engulfed them.

The violence of such catastrophes has been commented on by Professor Frank Hibber who, in describing the state of uncounted thousands of now extinct animals killed in Alaska during a prehistoric catastrophe, speaks of:

> ... thousands of animals killed in their prime ... animals torn apart and scattered over the landscape even though they may have weighed several tons ... violent storms might explain the peculiar finds of so many animals crammed in caverns and fissures from different geological periods ...

He further notes the layers of volcanic ash interspersed through the piles of bones and tusks of the slaughtered animals, with its implication of extreme heat and suffocation by volcanic gases.

Professor Immanuel Velikovsky, the historian and astronomer, whose theories about the cause of catastrophism in ancient times caused a major scientific upheaval in the 1950s, the ripples of which are still apparent, has vividly expressed this sudden death in common of animals:

> ... In the hills of Montreal and New Hampshire and in Michigan, five and six hundred feet above sea level, bones of whales have been found. In many places on the earth —on all continents—bones of sea animals and polar land animals and tropical animals have been found in great melees; so also in the Cumberland Cave in Maryland in the Chou Kou Tien fissure in China, and in Germany and Denmark. Hippopotamuses and ostriches were found together with seals and reindeer ... from the Arctic to the Antarctic ... in the high mountains and in the deep seas —we find innumerable signs of great upheavals, ancient and recent ...

Professor Velikovsky further points out in his book *Earth in*

Upheaval that Charles Darwin, writing of his travels in South America during the early part of the last century, noted that most of the extinct South American animals were contemporaneous with the sea shells found on the land. In considering the extermination of whole species in the area he writes:

... The mind at first is irresistibly hurried into the belief of some great catastrophe; but thus to destroy animals, both large and small, in southern Patagonia, in Brazil, on the Cordillera of Peru, in North America up to Bering Strait, *we must shake the entire framework of the globe*.

We know that the Arctic and Antarctic regions were once warm, that the Sahara was once a sea, that there are underwater evidences of what were once forests in the North Sea and off the coast of Peru, and that the highest mountains in the world, the Himalayas, show, by the presence of sea shells and mollusks, that they were once underwater.

If a made-made civilization had been overwhelmed, on one or several occasions, by the same sort of catacylsmic disaster which destroyed animals and forests and changed land and sea levels in various parts of the world, we might well expect to find recognizable vestiges of such cultures of pre-cataclysmic man. Some of these remains may already be known to us; the key lies in recognizing them.

One such collection of ruins may be those of Tiahuanaco, located at such a height that it seems inconceivable that a population large enough to construct such a city could ever have lived there—Tiahuanaco itself having an altitude of 12,500 feet, while some of the stone agricultural terraces, built around the sides of the surrounding mountains, climb to an incredible height, that of the perpetual snowline at more than 18,000 feet. Other undated ruins, some located deep beneath the oceans and seas, have an evident similarity with Tiahuanaco; whenever they were built they could not have been located at their present level in regard to the sea.

It is not necessary to remind ourselves that man, unlike

other species caught in prehistoric catastrophes, did not disappear, but simply went temporarily 'underground,' taking shelter in caves or on hilltops, or riding out the disturbance in ships or arks. Survivors of such destruction all over the world were able, moreover, to relay to succeeding generations something of the experiences through which they had passed, first by oral legend and subsequently by written records.

The majority of these legends, while conserving a certain unanimity about the occurrence of a world-wide flood and coincidental visitations of earthquakes, fire, and great tidal waves, mix physical observations with the wildest fantasy. Other destruction legends, however, contain certain features which are easily understandable in terms of certain modern theories about the ice ages, seismic disturbances and land changes due to the modification of the earth's crust.

There is, for example, a curious description of the Great Flood in Genesis when it is said (Genesis 7:19): '... on the same day were all the fountains of the great deep broken up and the windows of heaven were opened ...' The reference to 'the fountains of the great deep' suggests that the waters were rising from sources in addition to the diluvial rains. If the retreat of the last glaciation occurred about 12,000 years ago, as is generally accepted, and if it were considerably accelerated and accompanied by tempest and seismic disorders, this notation from the Bible, suggesting a filling from below as well as from above, becomes not religious fantasy but rather apt reporting of a phenomenon that some witnesses may have seen and remembered. The Koran, whether from a common or independent source, also records: '... The earth's surface seethed—the ark moved ... amid waves like mountains ...'

Besides the memory of the Great Flood preserved by almost all ancient nations and tribes, legends throughout the world refer to periodic destruction by fire and ice, earthquakes and sinkings, often with similar details. One of the Aztec codices, the codex Chimalpopoca, in describing one of the recurring catastrophes preserved in race memory related:

... The third sun is called *Quia-Tonatiuh*, sun of rain,

194

because there fell a rain of fire; all which existed burned; and there fell a rain of gravel. They also relate that while the sandstone, which we now see scattered about, and the *tetzontli* (basaltic rock) boiled with great tumult, there also rose the rocks of vermilion color ... This was in the year *Ce-Tecpatl*, One Flint, it was the day *Nahui-Quiahuitl*, Fourth Rain. Now, in this day, in which men were lost and destroyed in a rain of fire; the sun itself was on fire, and everything, together with the houses, was consumed ...

An Aztec preservation prayer to the god Tezcatlipoca, translated at the time of the conquest, contains recognizable allusions to earthquakes and fire from the sky, a frequent phenomenon remembered and mentioned by numerous other ancient peoples. The prayer, a long plea to the god for him to cease punishing mankind, which 'is leveled down and destroyed,' asks rather petulantly:

   ... Is it possible that this lash and chastisement is not given for our correction and amendment, but only for our total destruction and obliteration; that the sun shall never more shine upon us, but that we must remain in perpetual darkness and silence ... ?

After describing in detail the shaking and burning of the world, it concludes:

   ... universal master, let the sport and satisfaction thou hast already taken in this past punishment suffice; make an end of this smoke and fog of thy resentment; quench also the burning and destroying fire of thine anger; let serenity come and clearness; let the small birds of thy people begin to sing again and approach the sun; give them quiet weather ...

The *Popul Vuh* of the Mayas tells of how 'the gods moved mountains ... small and great mountains moved ...'

Again, in another surviving Mayan document, the book of

Chilam Balaam, there is a passage which not only describes a catastrophe, but contains an allusion to former lands sinking beneath the sea:

> During the Eleventh Ahau Catoun it occurred ... when the Earth began to waken. And a fiery rain fell, and ashes fell, and rocks and trees fell down. And their Great Serpent was ravished from the heavens. And then, in one watery blow, came the waters ... the sky fell down and the dry land sank. And in a moment the great annihilation was finished.
>
> And the Great Mother Seiba rose amidst recollections of the destruction of the earth.

Ovid, in his *Metamorphoses*, mentions some thought-provoking details in the following excerpts from his description of the conflagration of Phaëton, which itself may constitute a remembered record of an earlier catastrophe:

> ... Great cities perish, together with their fortifications, and the flames turn whole nations into ashes; woods, together with mountains, are on fire ... Aetna burns intensely with redoubled flames, and Parnassus, with its two summits, and Eryx ... Caucasus is on fire, and Ossa with Pindus, and Olympus, greater than them both, and the lofty Alps, and the cloud-bearing Alpennines ... Then was Libya made dry by the heat, the moisture being carried off ...

One is reminded of the observation, allegedly made by the Egyptian priests of Saïs to Solon regarding this same incident, described by Plato in *Timaeus*, referring to the same myth retold by Ovid:

> ... this has the form of a myth, but really signifies a declination of the bodies moving around the earth and in the heavens, and a great conflagration of things upon the earth recurring at long intervals of time: when this happens,

196

those who live upon the mountains and in dry and lofty places are more liable to destruction than those who dwell by rivers or on the sea-shore ...

Numerous ancient references to fire, destruction, darkness, the shaking of the earth, and erratic behaviour of other planets and comets have been explained by Professor Immanuel Velikovsky in his controversial *Worlds in Collision* and subsequent books as being records of violent catastrophes between the fifteenth and eighth centuries B.C., during which time intersection of planetary orbits brought about planetary collisions, causing comets, one of which became the planet Venus, after colliding with Mars. The earth, according to Dr. Velikovsky's theory, passed twice through the tail of such a comet with all the disastrous effects of enormous tides, earthquakes, barrages of hot stones, flows of lava and raising or lowering of parts of the surface of the earth. In the words of Sir Harold Spencer Jones, once the British Astronomer Royal:

... These various encounters are supposed to have been responsible for repeated changes in the earth's orbit, in the inclination of its axis, and in the lengths of the day, the seasons and the year. The earth on one occasion is supposed to have turned completely over, so that the sun rose in the west and set in the east. Dr. Velikovsky argues that between the fifteenth and eighth centuries B.C. the length of the year was 360 days and that it suddenly increased to 365¼ days in 687 B.C. The orbit of the moon and the length of the months were also changed ...

Numerous recorded occurrences of ancient times fit in with Professor Velikovsky's explanation, especially that of the relative newness of the planet Venus and of the change of calendar which occurred in antiquity on both sides of the ocean, with a revised Assyrian-Babylonian calendar year *and* the Mayan year both starting on a date equivalent, in our calculations, to February 26. The recording of shocks to the earth, of prolonged darkness, and even of the sun 'standing still,' as mentioned in Joshua—was noted by the Greek historian, Herodotus, who said that the priests of Memphis, Egypt, had told him, as a proof of the antiquity of their race, comprising 341 generations during 11,000 years that, during the ancient annals of Egyptian Kings 'the sun had risen several times where it customarily set and had set where it should have risen.' Careening of the earth under duress or a near hit by a comet, may be recorded in the tomb of Senmut, an Egyptian architect of the XVIII Dynasty, where a decorative ceiling painting shows the constellation of Orion travelling in an opposite direction to its normal path.

Allusions contained in the *Elder Edda*, a collection of Old Norse lengendary poems, concerning the giant cosmic Wolf of Destruction, Fenris, may concern racial memories of the comet predicted by Dr. Velikovsky. Such excerpts as: '... The Wolf devours the sun ... the other wolf devours the moon ... mountains will topple down when the Fenris wolf gets loose ... the Fenris wolf advances with wide open mouth; the upper jaw reaches to heaven and the lower jaw is on the earth ... the heavens are rent in two ...' are more easily understood when considered as primitive observations of earth shaking events in the skies.

These catastrophes of human recollection, substantiated by scientific theory and observation, included, among others, cataclysmic events specifically dated by Dr. Velikovsky as having occurred twenty-seven and thirty-four centuries ago, catastrophes consisting of, in the words of Dr. Velikovsky:

... hurricanes of global magnitude, of forests burning and swept away, of dust, stones, fire, and ashes falling from the sky, of mountains melting like wax, of lava flowing from riven ground, of boiling seas, of bituminous rain, of shaking ground and destroyed cities, of humans seeking refuge in caverns and fissures of the rock in the mountains, of oceans upheaved and falling on the land, of tidal waves moving toward the poles and back, of land becoming sea by submersion and the expanse of sea turning into desert, islands born and other drowned ... of changed climates, of displaced cardinal points and altered latitudes, of disrupted calendars, and of sundials and water clocks that point to changed length of day, month, and year, of a new polar star ...'

Dr. Velikovsky's first book *Worlds in Collision* caused an unprecedented uproar and protest on the part of various scientific disciplines, especially astronomers, in 1950, even before it appeared. When the book did make its appearance reviews oscillated between two extremes as, for example: 'The most amazing example of shattering of accepted concepts on record.' and : 'The worst book since the invention of movable characters.' At least one of the distinguished astronomers who opposed the book stated that the book was nothing but lies, adding paradoxically that he 'had not read and never would read' the book. Finally, threats from university professors to boycott other books published by Macmillan, the company that originally published *Worlds in Collision*, and various ultimata from scientists demanding cessation of publication, caused Macmillan to turn over publication to another company, Doubleday, which had a stronger policy against threats and, one may conclude, a stiffer backbone.

The controversy about Velikovsky's theories has continued for more than twenty years and, strangely, several of his astronomical theories or projections recently have been proved by space probes—particularly his remarkable prediction of the surface temperature of Venus at 800° Fahrenheit (Einstein estimated it at minus 25 degrees). His theory that Venus rotates in the opposite direction from the other planets, that the atmosphere of Venus is composed of carbohydrates and that the surface of Mars would be, like the moon, covered by craters, all of which have proved to be exactly true. An even more unusual theory that is becoming accepted is the positive and negative electric charges of the sun and of the planets.

Hugh Auchincloss Brown, a proponent of a theory of recurrent catastrophes (cataclysms of the Earth), interprets certain of the cataclysms of the past as being caused when the poles of figure (magnetic) move away from the poles of spin (axial), causing the earth to wobble on its axis until it realigns its axis and spins again like a giant top. He indicates that the earth has been rotating on its present axis for about 7000 years, causing the southern icecap to have increased to its present weight of 19 quadrillion tons—posing an interesting problem or choice, if we have one—either the ice will get heavier and eventually unbalance the axis of the earth, or it will melt and flood the world with a new water level 300 feet higher than it is at present, drowning the ports and lowlands of the present world as a like rising of the waters may have done in a former one.

This theory of a careening world of Professor Brown finds an eerie echo in a Hopi Indian legend concerning the end of one of the preceding worlds. Sotuknung, the first creation and Legate of the Creator, destroyed the Second World by commanding a pair of giant twins to leave their posts at the North and South Axial Poles, where they were stationed to keep the earth rotating. When they left their stations, the world lost balance, spun around, and rolled over twice. As retold by Frank Waters (*Book of the Hopi*):

> Mountains plunged into seas with a great splash, seas and lakes sloshed over the land; and as the world spun through lifeless space it froze into solid ice. This was the end of the Second World ... all the elements that had comprised the Second World were ... frozen into ice ... lifeless except for the people in their underground world ...

The memory of ice ages, preserved in the memory of so many tribes, suggests that the ice ages were somehow connected with, or the cause of, periodic catastrophes suffered by the earth. In the opinion of Hugh Auchincloss Brown: '... The present ice cap on Antarctica is merely the last of many ... that have previously existed ... the successor to a long lineage of glistening assassins of former civilizations on this planet ...' If this be the case, a most fruitful field for archaeological survey and exploration might be the Antarctic continent itself, although such a project is presently impossible, not only because of the depths of the glacier, but because it is still growing, a fact of ominous suggestion for the future. The snow and ice level is rising with such rapidity that 100-foot towers erected in the Antarctic by the Byrd expedition relatively few years ago are now almost covered to the top by snow and ice.

However, while there is general agreement that three or more probably four ice ages have occurred within the last million years, ending about 11,500 years ago, their cause still remains something of a mystery and as yet explainable only by theories. J. K. Charlesworth, an authority on glaciology at Queen's University, Belfast, has observed, concerning the origin of the ice ages: '... The cause of all these changes, one of the greatest riddles in geological history, remains unsolved ... the cause still eludes us ...'

Charles Hapgood, following a widely held theory that the poles have shifted many times, ascribes cataclysmic appearances to volcanic eruptions resulting from stress and strain below the earth's crust. The ice ages would then result from different positions of the poles, which would come from a slipping of the earth's outer crust, the outer shell of this crust being only 30 to 40 miles thick. The shifting of the crust resulting in new positions of the poles would bring about long periods of intense volcanic upheavals and the glaciers, according to this theory, would be the result, as well as the partial cause, of such climatic and seismic changes. This would also seemingly explain the fact that extremely unlikely places on the earth's surface, such as Africa and India, have been under glacier drift while other likely places, such as Siberia, have been free.

A key word in Professor Hapgood's theory is 'isostasy,' meaning approximately an equilibrium or equalization of pressure and applicable to the earth with its relatively weak crust, in that if too much material is concentrated in one spot, such as the pole with ever-increasing ice, the weak undercrust flows out from under as the crust gives way under stress, seeking a new isostatic adjustment or isostatic rebound. In addition, the rotating earth is not a true sphere, having a bulge at the equator and being slightly flattened at the poles; its true shape perhaps being best expressed as a 'triaxial ellipsoid,' with a progressive tendency for shortening of the radius and circumference of the earth at the higher latitudes, resulting in the thrusting up or tilting of sections of the earth's crust under stress, with the possibility of raising coasts, mountains and islands, as well as sinking coastlines, archipelagoes and even continents. In other words, cataclysms or severe earthquakes occurring even today on land and the continued oscillations or rising and falling of the floors of the oceans may be a perfectly normal procedure of the earth, although hardly a comfortable thought to the dwellers upon it.

A theory of catastrophism related to electric charges and the magnetism of the earth has been advanced by Dr. Manson Valentine, archaeologist and zoologist, and a supporter of the theory of recurrent cataclysms in the history of earth and man. In the course of his many expeditions to Central and South America and the Pacific islands he has personally studied the results of cataclysms, such as the protracted flooding and extrusions of caves, the sinking, tilting and lifting of coastlines and mountains. He has identified human artifacts within the raised lines of shells, in 'cross bedding of sand and sea flora including woven cotton threads, traces of fishnets and pottery in banks hundreds of feet above sea level in Paracas, Peru, and in the scars of tidal waves with accompanying sea debris in Ancon, Peru. The former is but one of the many instances of beaches throughout the world having been raised to heights over the present sea level such as has occurred in South America, Greenland, and Northern California.

Dr. Valentine's theory about the magnetic factor in cataclysmic change has not previously been published and is reproduced here in his own words:

One theory accountable for a possible cause of catastrophism on this planet seems not to have received the serious consideration it deserves. This factor does not concern itself with mechanical or astronomical collision with foreign bodies or matter in any form; rather, it involves periodic adjustments in the earth's polarity, secondarily affecting its rotation or solar orbit or both.

Anomalies in the magnetic field of our solar system, whether cyclic or sporadic, most certainly would create precataclysmic warnings here on earth. The onset of conditionings heralding such a cosmic event would, in all probability, be reflected in an ever widening discrepancy between the geographical positions of the earth's rotational and its magnetic poles. As the gap increases (a situation now in effect) magnetic stresses could conceivably be built up to the breaking point when swift compensatory polar readjustments would ensue. These shiftings would unquestionably result in catastrophic changes of the earth's crust. The four glaciations at regularly decreasing intervals during the Pleistocene could indicate a sort of periodicity for such violent events.

Electricity, familiar and of supreme importance to all of us, is credited by Dr. Valentine with a substantial influence in the the past and future of the earth. He suggests that the shifting or reversing of the poles may be due to magnetic tensions and stress built up within a gigantic generator—the earth itself.

In considering some apparently unexplainable electromagnetic phenomena of the present, he points out that the last discernible landmark on the planet's surface, which the astronauts in Apollo 12 were able to identify, was the strange 'white water' of the Bahama Banks.

... The wide swaths of this highly refractive material have been theoretically disposed of as caused by the riling of the marly bottom by fish, tidal currents etc., but that could not possibly explain their long persistence, their luminosity or the fact that they are surrounded by a sort of halo suggestive of an electrical phenomenon or magnetic field ...

Electromagnetic anomalies in the same area, in the opinion of Dr. Valentine, may explain the occurrences within the

Bermuda Triangle, a triangular area roughly between Bermuda, Puerto Rico, and the Bahamas, comprising approximately the western third of the Sargasso Sea, where hundreds of ships and aircraft have disappeared through the years, from the USS *Cyclops* with a crew of three hundred in 1918 to the recent and well-documented incident of December 5, 1945, when a complete flight of five U.S. Navy planes radioed that they were having compass and directional difficulties and then disappeared, along with the large flying boat sent to their rescue. Concerning the possible electromagnetic deviations, Dr. Valentine recounts:

> ... Compasses spin like tops unaccountably at certain times and over certain spots. I myself have witnessed this eerie sight near Moselle shoal, in deep water. Sometimes a malfunctioning of both the magnetic and gyro compasses will presage the weird experience of a 'white out,' when a vessel in a dead calm, without benefit of fog or other meteorological aberrations, will lose sight of the horizon, the sun or another boat in tow. Both sea and aircraft, some of respectable size, have been known to disappear ... Suffice to say that such untoward events may not be totally unconnected with a state of relative magnetic instability centered in the islands. If such were the case, and it seems quite likely, then it follows that seismic activity, involving the intricate system of faults throughout the Bahamas ...

Whatever has been the cause of the violent modifications of the earth's climate, surface, and inhabitants in the past, we now stand at a stage in our own development where, possibly not for the first time in man's history, he has had the ability to considerably modify, for good or evil, his surrounding environment. There are constant references in ancient legends to man's prior destruction—not only that men had become evil and incurred the wrath of the gods or god, but also that those about to be destroyed had developed powers of their own that angered heaven.

Certain of these legends find an echo in the readings of

Edgar Cayce, including the growth of an advanced science that developed along different although not less destructive lines than ours. A reference of his to the uses of power from and the destructive potentialities of what he calls 'crystals' find an odd corroboration in ancient legends (an inference not lost on those who speculate on the reasons for the compass and electromagnetic deviations in the Bermuda Triangle), which it is doubtful that Cayce had ever heard of although, while in a trance, he described the crystals and their attributed location in considerable detail.

In the purely scientific approach of today, legends, unexplained evidences of ancient knowledge, historical anachronisms, inexplicable artifacts and existing ruins, coincidences in unrelated languages, past geological catastrophes, the worldwide spread and periodic destruction of animal life, the backward extension of the age of man, and finally ESP and race memory, the existence of Atlantis or other sunken lands, is not going to be accorded general acceptance by the scientific disciplines. The problem is not only related to rewriting textbooks but also concerns the insularity of outlook shared by many who like to consider the history of man and the world in well-ordered predictable patterns—which it never is.

As we delve farther back into the past of the world we find, as is to be expected, things that we did not suspect to have existed—and now, with tools of increased efficiency at our command, we may be about to come upon some surprising things, not all of which will be logical to our outlook or complimentary to our ego. Some of these discoveries may already be fairly evident but have somehow not been recognized.

In the case of Atlantis—using the word for one or more advanced cultures prior to our own—if a splendid sunken city were found at the bottom of the Atlantic Ocean, or even if a submarine quake precipitated it to the surface, scientific skepticism would probably still not permit it to be accepted as Atlantis, but would probably label it, as suggested by Charles Boland, as a sunken Greek shipment of building materials.

In any case, the increasing tempo of undewater discoveries, the possibility of finding new written records, re-examining existing ones and even breaking undeciphered scripts, as well as new techniques of dating, will bring about reassessments of the past prehistory.

Exploration under the ice and at the bottom of the sea may bring to light artifacts that will put a new aspect on the past before the past. As archaeological expeditions are costly and difficult to organize for so extensive a field as the ocean bottom, despite the excellent coring, current, and depth studies by oceanic research organizations, archaeology may be considerably furthered in the future by finds occasioned by naval undersea manoeuvres or by deep-sea probes for oil. Salt domes, indicative of oil and natural gas as well as the one time presence of land above water have been located in the Mid-Atlantic Ridge. It should also be added that the search and need for oil could also cause considerable and perhaps cumulative unfreezing of the polar icecap in the event that a super 450,000-ton tanker should founder on a polar route with its oil cargo. The resultant melting, it has been calculated, would leave shorelines of the world again under water, as happened circa 10,000 years ago, with the melting of the last glaciation, in a sort of cosmic 'this is where we came in' replay of cataclysmic events.

It can be pointed out, of course, that our present culture stands in danger of extinction because of man-made dangers and activities undertaken without consideration for his own survival, while the disappearance of former cultures was due to natural calamities. And yet, even this assumption, in the light of certain records and evidences from the past, leaves an opening for a tantalizing doubt.

CHAPTER TWELVE

WARNINGS FROM THE DISTANT PAST

The destructive potential of scientific technology is no secret to the generations of man now inhabiting a planet menaced not only by the dangers inherent in an unstable cosmos, but also by disasters and possibly final doom paradoxically brought about by our own advances in science and by our own growing understanding of the universe. The thought suggests itself, therefore, that, given the long-time presence on this planet of a civilized race before the apparent start of our own civilization, a race, moreover, whose mental ability, as calculated by estimated brain capacity, in measuring surviving skulls of the Crô-Magnon man, was equal or *superior* to our own, the descendants of this, or a more or less contemporaneous race may have developed a science, which while not analogous to ours and taking perhaps a different road, might have nevertheless arrived at the same final impasse.

Certain hints, while proving nothing conclusively, serve to awaken reflective thoughts. In southern Iraq, in the Euphrates Valley, in the course of an exploratory digging in 1947, layers of culture were successfully penetrated by what one might call an archaeological mine shaft. Starting from the present level, the excavation passed the ancient city culture levels of Babylonia, Chaldea, and Sumeria, flood levels between different ages of city culture, then the village level, subsequently that of primitive farmers, at a time level of 8000 years ago, while below that herdsman culture and finally a period corresponding to the Magdalenian or cave culture. At the bottom of all levels, a floor of fused glass was revealed, similar to nothing else except the desert floor in New Mexico after the blasts which inaugurated our present Atomic Era.

Vitrified soil, of the type caused by atomic explosion, has also been found in the Gobi desert.

Dr. Vyacheslar Zaitser, a Russian philologist of the Byelo-Russian Academy of Science, as reported in the recent book *Psychic Discoveries Behind the Iron Curtain*, makes a judicious observation about a biblical event familiar to us all. 'The Biblical account of the destruction of Sodom and Gomorrah,' he says, 'resembles a nuclear explosion as it would be described by an uneducated witness.'

These reports do not necessarily signify, of course, that there were atomic wars on earth before our own. They may simply mean that the earth has been struck from time to time by a meteor or asteroid considerably larger than the usual meteors that occasionally penetrate our atmosphere. Such a heavenly bomb might have formed Crater Lake, Colorado; or what has been called the '1908 Hiroshima' when a cataclysm blast, thought to have been caused by a meteorite, rocked Siberia, occurring northeast of Lake Baikal, killing a herd of 1500 reindeer, flattening forests and leaving vestiges of radio-activity around its crater to the present day.

There is, however, another semi-historical indication of catastrophic destruction initiated and caused by man or gods acting like men, which is recorded in the *Mahabharata*, sometimes called the *Iliad* of ancient India (but over eight times as long as Homer) and therefore more comprehensive and also explicit in detail. The *Mahabharata* is essentially a huge compendium of religious teachings, customs, history and legends concerning the gods and heroes of ancient India. It is also considered to contain elements pertaining to the conquest of India by the Aryan invaders from the north who invaded and conquered northern India several thousand years ago and probably destroyed, among other cities, Harappa and Mohenjo-Daro in the Indus Valley. This extremely ancient collection of books probably encompasses other records and legends current in the ancient period during which it was compiled.

The *Mahabharata*, written in Sanskrit, is perhaps one of the most ancient religious and literary texts still in use today and, like the Bible which contains numerous references to historic events of countries neighboring to Israel, the Hindu classic may preserve bits of information from an older world that are not only picturesque but sometimes rather alarming.

When western students first began to study and comment on the *Mahabharata* during the period of British rule in India, certain detailed references to ancient air ships (*vimanas*) including even how to construct them and how they were powered, matter of fact descriptions of controlled fire power in warfare, rockets, and even the 'arrow of unconsciousness' (*mohanastra*) which rendered armies helpless. Early scholars customarily considered these references, decades before the invention of airplanes or poison gas, as poetic hyperbole and were accustomed, in the words of V. Ramachandra Dikshitar, '... to glibly characterize everything found in this literature as imagination and summarily dismiss it as unreal ...'

Students of the Victorian era would, of course, have little understanding or feeling of coincidence in descriptions of 'two story sky chariots with many windows' blazing with red flame 'that race up into the sky until they look like comets,' or ships that 'soared into the air to the regions of both the sun and the stars.'

A gigantic English prose translation of the *Mahabharata* was made by an Indian scholar, P. Chandra Roy, in the latter part of the nineteenth century, aided by funds from the Government of India, several of the Maharajas, and other individual sources. This translator seemed to have a curious reaction to some of the descriptions of total warfare, remarking in one of his introductions that he, as a Brahmin (of the priestly caste) and not a Kshatriya (of the warrior caste) could not fully appreciate or approve of the descriptions of total carnage he was translating but judged them to be necessary to the masterpiece as a whole, especially as it concerned the actions of the gods.

Some of these descriptions may have been enigmatical to scholars of the last century who read and translated them but they are not especially mysterious or hard to understand to

209

almost anyone alive today or who may still be alive in an uncertain future. The following excerpts from the *Mahabharata* and the *Ramanyana* are startlingly familiar to us in spite of the thousands of intervening years, telling of:

A single projectile charged with all the power of the Universe. An incandescent column of smoke and flame, as bright as ten thousand Suns, rose in all its splendour ...

... it was an unknown weapon, an iron thunderbolt, a gigantic messenger of death which reduced to ashes the entire race of the Vrishnis and the Andhakas.

... The corpses were so burned as to be unrecognizable. Their hair and nails fell out; pottery broke without any apparent cause, and the birds turned white. After a few hours, all foodstuffs were infected.

And especially the following:

... to escape from this fire the soldiers threw themselves in streams to wash themselves and all their equipment ...

The destruction of the enemy army by the 'iron thunderbolt' (certainly a more logical name than the 'Fat Man' dropped on Nagasaki) is described in the following excerpt from the *Samsaptaka-Badha Parva* of the *Drona Parva* in an effective and poetic manner:

... Then Vayu (the presiding deity of that mighty weapon) bore away crowds of Samsaptakas with steeds and elephants and cars and weapons, as if these were dry leaves of trees ... Borne away by the wind, O King, they looked highly beautiful like flying birds ... flying away from trees ...'

And again, in the *Naryanastra Mokshana Parva* (*Drona Parva*), reference is made to the 'Agneya weapon' incapable of being resisted by the very gods.

Meteors flashed down from the firmament ... A thick gloom suddenly shrouded the host. All points of the compass were enveloped by that darkness ... Inauspicious winds began to blow ... the sun seemed to turn round, the universe, scorched with heat, seemed to be in a fever. The elephants and other creatures of the land, scorched by the energy of that weapon, ran in flight ... The very waters being heated, the creatures residing in that element began to burn ... hostile warriors fell down like trees burnt down in a raging fire—huge elephants burnt by that weapon, fell down on the earth ... uttering fierce cries ... other(s) scorched by the fire ran hither and thither, as in the midst of a forest conflagration, the steeds ... and the cars (chariots) also, burnt by the energy of that weapon looked ... like the tops of trees burnt in a forest fire ...

The after effects to the earth, one might infer, noted by some ecologist of prehistory:

... winds dry and strong and showering gravel blew from every side ... Birds began to wheel making circles ... The horizon on every side seemed to be covered with fog. Meteors—showering blazing coals fell on the earth from the sky ... The Sun's disk ... seemed to be always covered with dust ... Fierce circles of light were seen every day around both the sun and the moon ... A little while after the Kuru king, Yudhishshira heard of the wholesale carnage of the Vrishnis in consequence of the iron bolt ... (*Mausala Parva*)

Even a prayer to the Creator has come down to us, imploring divine intercession to stop the effects of the 'final' weapon:

... O illustrious one—let the threefold universe—the future, the Past and the Present exist. From thy wrath a substance like fire has sprung into existence; even now blistering hills, trees and rivers and all kinds of herbs and grass in the mobile and immoble universe is being reduced to ashes! (*Abhimanyu Badha Parva*)

A most unusual excerpt from the *Mausala Parva* contains

211

an oddly modern reminder relative to limitation, destruction and disposal of deadly missiles:

> ... an iron bolt through which all the individuals in the race of the Vrishnis and Andhakas became consumed into ashes ... a fierce iron bolt that looked like a gigantic messenger of death ... In great distress of mind the King caused that iron bolt to be reduced into fine powder. Men were employed, O King, to cast that powder into the sea ...

Such strangely detailed reports, which make sense to us, but not at all to the first translator, must be considered in context of the times, spirit, and outlook of those who wrote them. Ancient peoples, living in the 'age of miracles,' took all sorts of magical occurrences for granted and, above all, considered civilization to be a stream, a flux and reflux of cultures rather than a continuous march forward. Scientific marvels or prophecies were simply noted and recorded as they found them, without any attempt at corroboration or thought that they might be re-examined in the light of actually having occurred by future generations.

What is the meaning of these numerous references? We are aware that ancient literature of different parts of the earth customarily contain extraordinary flights of fancy and incredible legends which may, nonetheless, refer to an imaginative version of something that once really happened. However, when some of the more remarkable of these fantasies seem exactly to parallel a collection of scientific facts with which we are already nervously familiar, then we become aware of a case of historical *déjà vu* or 'we have passed this way before.'

All known history, and even such prehistory as we are able to reconstruct, seems to present us with a repetitive pattern as well as with an implied warning, for as a French saying expresses it: 'Those who ignore history are condemned to repeat it.'

Warfare is a basic fact of history and history itself has been classified as the history of those who won—the losers, especially in the far past, having completely disappeared, being absorbed or annihilated by the victors. Warfare in itself seems to be almost an inherited instinct, not necessarily economic, as the economic historians would have it, but from a desire to triumph in combat as members of a group, tribe, or nation against another group, tribe, or nation. In the known history of warfare up to the last few decades, this instinct, with its trappings of romance and excitement, could be more or less freely indulged in. Sometimes, as in the case of city states of ancient Mexico, warfare would be comfortably and efficiently planned and carried out to the satisfaction *and* preservation of the combatant states. In a rather charmingly named confrontation, 'The War of the Flowers' (*Xochi-yaoyotl*), two small equal armies would be pitted against each other by prearrangement until one of the two triumphed, and carried off the vanquished to sacrifice them to the gods to keep the delicate balance of tribute due to and benefits conferred by the lords of the skies. (One of the reasons for the Spanish victory against the Aztecs was that the Aztec warriors were trying to capture the Spaniards while the Spaniards were trying to kill as many Aztecs as possible.)

Up to the present era, neither warfare nor the effects of scientific technology had seriously affected the earth itself; no matter how great the carnage, humanity itself was never in danger. Even the depredations of the Mongols, while destroying whole populations and ruining canal systems without which the centers of Central Asia and Mesopotamia never regained their former population density, did not seriously endanger the world, however final their appearance on the horizon seemed to their adversaries. With what we know of history, it seems difficult to accept the possibility that any previous culture could have stumbled on means of general destruction that may have precipitated their own disappearance from the planet. Still the possibility was there for scientists or magicians of other ages to discover and the unusual references in the *Mahabharata*, perhaps incorporated into it from sources so dim that we cannot perceive them, are especially

213

notable in that we have only been able to understand the references to weapons described thousands of years ago as our own destructive techniques increase their 'overkill' potentialities.

For a poetic rendition of a fate that may eventually be awaiting us, we can turn to a stately prophecy from Roman times, from the stylus of the poet playwright Seneca:

> *A single day will see the burial of all mankind,*
> *All that the long forebearance of fortune has produced,*
> *All that has been raised to eminence,*
> *All that is famous and all that is beautiful,*
> *Great thrones, great nations—*
> *All will descend into one abyss,*
> *All will be overthrown in one hour ...*

Another poetic suggestion of future instant doom comes from the *Elder Edda*, an Icelandic saga, written long ago in an ancestor language of the present Scandinavian–Germanic group to which English also belongs. Excerpts from the Icelandic are less stately than the Latin, but somewhat more direct:

> *Dark grows the sun,*
> *Brothers shall fight and kill ...*
> *Axe-time, sword-time,*
> *Shields are sundered,*
> *Wind-time, wolf-time,*
> *Till the world falls dead.*

and again:

> *Mountains dash together ...*
> *And heaven is split in two,*
> *The sun grows dead—*
> *The earth sinks into the sea,*
> *The bright stars vanish*
> *Fires rage and raise their flames*
> *As high as heaven.*

We may wonder whether these messages of doom were written prophecies or memories and whether all the legends of destruction from the earth's most ancient peoples were truly legends or confused and embellished recollections of what their ancestors had experienced. And when, from a point of view so far back in time that we usually label it a marker of emerging civilization, we find uniquely exact descriptions of the effects of our most modern weapons, we wonder whether history is a repetition of vast concentric circles, as is usually expressed in the Oriental view of continuing and repeating cycles of civilization and life itself, rather than a constant march forward. If so, why study history at all, and especially vanished cultures so far off in time that we can only vaguely perceive them flickering like a star of lesser magnitude? But, besides the fascination of history, its undiscovered mysteries, its splendid vistas and its still largely unexplored epochs that seem to extend farther back in time, the study of vanished civilizations and the reasons for their disappearance has a negative value as well as a positive one, teaching us what *not* to do—so that we may ourselves survive.

ACKNOWLEDGMENTS

The author wishes to express his sincere appreciation to the following persons who have contributed advice, suggestions, expertise, photographs, or drawings to this book. Such mention in no way implies their acceptance or non-acceptance of the author's theories.

Special acknowledgment is made to the following:

Professor Charles Hapgood, cartographer, historian, writer, whose remarkable work in checking certain ancient maps for longitudinal coordinates represents a revolutionary and decisively important step in establishing the scientific advances of forgotten civilizations.

Dr. Ivan Sanderson, explorer, zoologist, writer, and tireless investigator whose investigation of unusual phenomena encompasses as well the unexplained mysteries of the past.

Further acknowledgment is made in alphabetical order.

S. Farooq Ali, Government of India Tourist Office

José María Bensaúde, President, Navecor Lines, Lisbon, Portugal

Valerie Berlitz, writer, artist

Anne Ware Bird, researcher of North American prehistory

Dr. Cyrus Bird, Curator of South American Archaeology, American Museum of Natural History

Hugh Lynn Cayce, President, Association for Research and Enlightenment

Dr. Gordon Ekholm, Curator of Mexican Archaeology, American Museum of Natural History

Marion Fawcett, author, researcher

Dr. Cyrus H. Gordon, historian, linguist, archaeologist

J. Silva Júnior, Director, 'Terra Nostra,' Azores islands
Theodora Kane, painter
Samir Khalil, writer, archaeologist
Constantine Mertvago, linguist, philologist
Howard Metz, pyramidologist
William Morris, lexicographer, columnist
Albert C. Muller, radiation engineer
Lcdo. Carlos M. Peralta, Consul-General of Costa Rica
Leon Pomerance, archaeologist
Dimitri Rebikoff, inventor, oceanographer, archaeologist
Wilbert O. Sánchez H., Mexican Government Tourist Bureau
Robert E. Silverberg, historian, author
Robert E. Stone, president, NEARA
Carl Payne Tobey, mathematician, astronomer, author, astrologer
Jack A. Ulrich, explorer, archaeologist
James Valentine, photographer, writer, ecologist
Joaquim De Vasconcelos, Portuguese Government information office
Dr. Immanuel Velikovsky, astronomer, historian, author, linguist

BIBLIOGRAPHY

Maps of the Ancient Sea Kings—Charles Hapgood—Philadelphia, 1966

Worlds in Collision—Immanuel Velikovsky—Victor Gollancz, 1950

Aku-Aku—Thor Heyerdahl—George, Allen & Unwin, 1958

Man Hunting in the Jungle—O. M. Dyott—Edward Arnold, 1929

Lost Trails Lost Cities—P. H. Fawcett—New York, 1953

Island at the Center of the World—S. Englert—New York, 1970

Technology in the Ancient World—Henry Hodges—Allen Lane—The Penguin Press, 1970

Sons of the Sun—Marcel F. Homet—Neville Spearman Ltd, 1963

Lost Languages—P. E. Cleater—Robert Hale, 1959

Mound Builders of Ancient America—Robert Silverberg—Connecticut, 1968

Les Empires de la Mer—Attilo Gaudio—Paris, 1962

The Mystery of Atlantis—Charles Berlitz—New York, 1969

Psychic Discoveries Behind the Iron Curtain—Sheila Ostrander and Lynn Schroeder—New Jersey, 1970

Old Civilizations of the New World—A. Hyatt Verrill—Williams & Norgate, 1929

Cataclysms of the Earth—Hugh Auchincloss Brown—New York, 1967

Lost Cities—Herman and Georg Schreiber—Weidenfeld & Nicolson, 1955

Lost Worlds of Africa—James Wellard—Hutchinsons, 1967

Realm of the Incas—Victor W. von Hagen—New American Library, 1957

World of the Maya—Victor W. von Hagen—New American Library, 1960

Earth Changes—The Edgar Cayce Foundation—Virginia, 1959

History Unearthed—Sir Leonard Woolley—Benn, 1963

Dead Cities and Forgotten Tribes—Gordon Cooper—Lutterworth Press, 1952

Stonehenge of the Kings—Patrick Crampton—John Baker, 1968

La Vida de los Mayas—Franz Blom—Mexico, 1944

Early Man—F. Clark Howell—New York, 1968

Le Livre du Mysterieux Inconnu—Robert Charroux—Paris, 1969

Histoire Inconnue des Hommes Depuis Cent Mille Ans—Robert Charroux—Paris, 1963

The Rock Pictures of Europe—Herbert Kuhn—Sidgwick & Jackson, 1956

Les Paladins du Monde Occidental—Laurence Talbot—Tangíers, 1965

Man, God and Magic—Ivar Lissner—Jonathan Cape, 1961

Tauchfahrt in die Vergangenheit—Hanns-Wolf Rackl—Germany, 1964

Voices in Stone—Ernst Doblhoffer—Souvenir Press, 1961

Earth in Upheaval—Immanuel Velikovsky—Victor Gollancz & Sidgwick & Jackson, 1955

Radio Carbon Dating—Willard E. Libby—C.U.P., 1952

The Ancient Mariners—Lionel Casson—Victor Gollancz, 1959

Book of the Hopi—Frank Waters—New York, 1969

The Silent Past—Ivar Lissner—Jonathan Cape, 1963

The Dawn of Magic—Pauwels and Bergier—Anthony Gibbs & Phillips, 1960

Flights into Yesterday—Leo Deuel—MacDonald, 1971

Life, Land and Water in Ancient Peru—Paul Kosok—New York, 1965

The Morning of Mankind—Robert Silverberg—World's Work, 1970

Easter Island—John Dos Passos—New York, 1971

The Velikovsky Affair—Alfred de Grazia—Sidgwick & Jackson, 1966

Ships, Shoals and Amphoras—Suzanne de Borhegyi—New York, 1961

The Underwater World—Jim Thorne—New York, 1969

Fair Gods and Stone Faces—Constance Irwin—W. H. Allen, 1963

They All Discovered America—Charles Michael Boland—New York, 1961

The Aztecs of Mexico—G. C. Vaillant—Penguin Books, 1965

The Broken Spears—edited by Miguel Leon-Portilla—Constable, 1962

Historia General de las Cosas de Nueva España—Fray Bernardino de Sahagun—Mexico, 1938

Inscripcões e Tradicões do América Pré-Histórica, Especialmente do Brasil—Bernardo Da Silva Ramos, R.—Rio de Janeiro, 1930–39

Edgar Cayce on Atlantis—Edgar Evans Cayce—New York, 1968

Ponape—Sibley S. Morrill—San Francisco, 1970

Cities in the Sea—Nicholas C. Flemming, New York, 1971

Runa Simita Yachay—Demetrio Tupac Yupanqui—Lima, 1961

Diccionario Quichua—Luis Cordero—Quito, 1955

Voyage to Atlantis—James W. Mavor, Jr.—Souvenir Press, 1969

Libro de las Atlántidas—Armando Vivante y J. Imbelloni—Buenos Aires, 1939

Diccionario Español-Maya—Dr. Ermilo Solis Alcala—Mexico, 1949

La Escultura Arquitectónica de Uxmal—Marta Foncerrada de Molina—Mexico, 1965

The Encylopedia of Oceanography—Rhodes Farbridge—Vam Nostrand Reinhold Co., 1967

The Mahabharata (English Translation)—Protap Chandra Roy—Calcutta, 1889

Diccionario de Aztequismos—Dr C. A. Robelo—Mexico, 1932

Men out of Asia—Harold Sterling Gladwin—New York, 1947

Before Columbus—Cyrus H. Gordon—New York, 1971

The Lost Americans—Frank C. Hibber—New York, 1946

The Path of the Pole—Charles Hapgood—New York, 1970

A History of Land Mammals in the Western Hemisphere—W. B. Scott—New York, 1937

Ecuador-Andean Mosaic—Rolf Blomberg—Stockholf, 1952

Autobiography of a Yogi—Paramhansa Yogananda—Rider & Co., 1955

Invisible Residents—Ivan Sanderson—New York, 1970

The Bible—King James Version

The Koran

MYSTERIES OF THE UNIVERSE—REVEALED

Charles Berlitz
Without a Trace   £1.50 ☐
The Mystery of Atlantis   £1.50 ☐
The Bermuda Triangle   £1.25 ☐

Charles Berlitz & William Moore
The Philadelphia Experiment   £1.25 ☐
The Roswell Incident   £1.25 ☐

Robert Chapman
Unidentified Flying Objects   £1.25 ☐

Tom Graves
Needles of Stone   £1.95 ☐

Hans Holzer
The Ufonauts   95p ☐

Major D E Keyhoe
Aliens From Space   75p ☐

All these books are available at your local bookshop or newsagent, and can be ordered direct from the publisher or from Dial-A-Book Service.

To order direct from the publisher just tick the titles you want and fill in the form below:

Name _____

Address _____

_____

Send to:
Granada Cash Sales
PO Box 11, Falmouth, Cornwall TR10 9EN

Please enclose remittance to the value of the cover price plus:

UK 45p for the first book, 20p for the second book plus 14p per copy for each additional book ordered to a maximum charge of £1.63.

BFPO and Eire 45p for the first book, 20p for the second book plus 14p per copy for the next 7 books, thereafter 8p per book.

Overseas 75p for the first book and 21p for each additional book.

To order from Dial-A-Book Service, 24 hours a day, 7 days a week:

Telephone 01 836 2641 – give name, address, credit card number and title required. The books will be sent to you by post.

DIAL-A-BOOK

Granada Publishing reserve the right to show new retail prices on covers, which may differ from those previously advertised in the text or elsewhere.